DIVORCE
LIVING THROUGH THE AGONY

Mary Kirk has worked as a journalist for over 15 years. In 1990 she trained as a relationships counsellor and counselled with C.M.A.C. (now called Marriage Care). She is the author of *The Marriage Work-Out Book* and co-author of *Holy Matrimony? An exploration of ministry and marriage.*

Mary Kirk is a Roman Catholic. She married in 1972, and has two daughters (born 1973, 1975). She was widowed in 1986. Mary was engaged to a divorcee in 1990, who also died before their planned marriage in 1991. This engagement, in breach of the 'rules' of the Catholic Church, meant she could no longer counsel for a Catholic organization, but she has remained in touch with Marriage Care, and *The Marriage Work-Out Book* was written with their cooperation.

Mary Kirk has worked extensively for both Anglican and Roman Catholic churches in a voluntary capacity, most recently in France for the Secours Catholique (Caritas France), working with the homeless and socially excluded.

For Peter

Divorce

Living Through the Agony

Mary Kirk

A LION BOOK

Published by
Lion Publishing plc
Sandy Lane West, Oxford, England
ISBN 0 7459 3804 3

First edition 1998
10 9 8 7 6 5 4 3 2 1 0

A catalogue record for this book is
available from the British Library

Printed and bound in Great Britain by
Caledonian International Book Manufacturing

Acknowledgments
The publishers would like to thank the following for permission to use
material in this book:
Extracts from *Women After Divorce: Preliminary report from a ten-year follow-up*
by Judith M. Wallerstein in the *American Journal of Orthopsychiatry* 56 [1],
January 1986. Copyright © 1986 by the American Orthopsychiatry
Association, Inc. Reproduced by permission.
Extracts from 'The Language of Love' in 'Parish Diary' by Pastor Ignotus, *The
Tablet*, 31 May 1997. Reproduced by permission of The Tablet Publishing Co.
Ltd.
Extracts from the Catechism of the Catholic Church © Geoffrey Chapman (an
imprint of Cassell plc). Used by permission.
'Can't live with you... or without you' by Toby Harnden from *Daily Telegraph*,
17 December 1994. Used by permission.
Extract by Ellenruth Susskind from *Jewish Chronicle*, 16 March 1984. Used by
permission of *Jewish Chronicle*.
Biblical quotes are taken from *The New English Bible* © 1961, 1970 Oxford
and Cambridge University Presses.

Acknowledgments

My gratitude goes primarily to the many divorced and separated people who were willing to share their experiences with me, both in person and in correspondence, with such courage. Of these, my thanks go especially to Tanya Palmer, who has allowed me to quote freely from the poems and short stories inspired by the breakup of her marriage, and to Frances Adburgham, who has contributed largely to my understanding of many of the issues.

I have been greatly helped by individual counsellors from the organizations Marriage Care (which also provided premises for interviewing) and Relate, by the Marriage and Partnership Research Charity One plus One, and personally by Dr Jack Dominian, Thelma Fisher, director of National Family Mediation, and the Rev. Tom Leary, director of St Luke's Couple Counselling Service.

This book would not have been possible without the help of my researcher David Kitton and the patience of Peter Hudson, to whom my heartfelt thanks also go.

MARY KIRK

Contents

Introduction

I always describe [my divorce] as if someone had put their hand down my throat and ripped my guts up.

'Divorce is a life sentence,' said one of the people interviewed for this book. Just as a wedding day is not a marriage, the decree absolute is rarely the end of the story. Many of those who spoke or wrote to the author about their experience of living with divorce felt that they could never be totally free of the effects of this trauma. The breakdown of the marriage, and its legal ending, coloured every area of their lives, current and future, sometimes many years on, placing constraints on their freedom to be the person they wished to be, or believed they had once been.

What does divorce mean?

Death is fate; divorce means failure to most.[1]

This view—that the form of bereavement that divorce imposes on one or both separating partners is more bitter and harder to endure than grief after the death of a spouse—seems almost universal among the divorced. The sense of inadequacy, failure, guilt, often with loathing and self-hatred intermingled, frequently differentiate these two great personal losses of adult life:

Although divorce is usually thought of as an event, it is probably more appropriate to view it as the catalyst for a series of negative life changes.[2]

And yet divorce, as a life event, lags behind decease of spouse in the 'stress league'.

There can be few people who have been through it who would say that divorce is merely a decree absolute, a piece of paper, a manumission which frees them into singleness again. The traces of conjugal living are not so easily erased. Divorce changes one's status, but there is no formal rite of passage to solemnize the termination of the relationship.

With the piece of paper comes a ratification of all that is imposed by separation—a change of behaviour and, for some women, a change of title. If it has not happened before, physical cohabitation comes to an end, as does economic inter-dependence and financial security, if it existed. For many—men and women—it spells emotional, sexual, social, and often economic deprivation. And if they are members of a church, there can sometimes be spiritual isolation as well, to add to the burden. Divorce will almost invariably mean troubles for the children of the union. Security and even respectability may disappear. Shame and failure are predominant emotions. Sometimes there is the gall of knowing that the erstwhile spouse is rushing to the registry office with a new partner, all too swiftly acquiring new intimacy, home, family and status.

And yet there is no ready-made social support. No ritual exists to untie the knot, to ease the formality into reality. Unless contested, it can happen (in the absence of the protagonists) in small strip-lit courtrooms up and down the country, their names figuring on an often long list of those who now find the pain of living together greater than the pain of living apart. Their personal investment in matrimony has not paid off.

One of the pleas of this book will be for some rite of passage to formalize and mark this transition from married to not married.

Divorce today

'Bitter custody battle over eight hanging baskets'

'Unfaithful wife has husband evicted'

'Row over custody of Labrador'

'Wife demands chef and butler in divorce deal'

Thus human tragedy is reduced to a headline for our amusement over the breakfast table. It appeals to a rather shameful sense of superiority, *schadenfreude*—a certain satisfaction in others' misfortunes. While this book was being written there was a newspaper report that a TV company plans a 'cruel and bitchy' gameshow in which separated or divorced couples will meet and compete in the name of entertainment— as though the divorced were some sort of freaks of nature, objects of ridicule and fun—so that we can sit smugly watching and say, 'That won't happen to me.'

But it can and does:

When I had heard programmes about divorce (on the radio, for instance), I had felt sorry for the people concerned but never for a moment thought this would one day happen to me.

There is no longer anything unusual in divorce. Many hundreds of thousands of us will know and share the experience, for we are a divorcing nation. England and Wales now have the highest divorce rate in Europe. The Office of Population Censuses and Surveys (OPCS) announced in 1996 that more than half the couples marrying that year were unlikely to make it to their Silver Wedding, and—if current rates continued—one in nine couples would divorce before their fifth wedding anniversary, and almost one in four before their tenth.

A marriage, according to the Central Statistical Office, now lasts for an average of just under ten years, but almost one in ten breaks up before the second anniversary. In the early 1990s the Society of Wedding Photographers took the precaution of charging a 'divorce deposit' in case the newly-weds split before the photos were ready. Of existing marriages 41 per cent were expected to break down, compared with an estimate of 37 per cent in 1987, and 34 per cent in 1980.

Divorce is therefore big business for the lawyers, and when it involves the rich and famous—especially the royal—it provokes column kilometres rather than column centimetres in the press. When lawyers and journalists move in, things are apt to get expensive and nasty:

> The solicitors were ready to pounce and set their 'fees clock' ticking at the earliest possible moment. I believe that in our case they were too eager to set their wheels in motion.

Perhaps there is some excuse for the TV company's lack of taste and sensitivity. Royal and celebrity divorce has set a trend for a very public airing of grievances, though the spin off of that is that marital breakdown provokes less social stigma than it once did; we have, in general, lost the horror of it. The sheer weight of numbers itself has made the splitting of a household more acceptable. *Debrett*, the arbiter and barometer of social acceptability, brought out its first guide to manners in fifteen years in 1996[3] with a completely revised section on the etiquette of divorce, remarriage and step-families.

There are many factors contributing to the enormous rise in divorce which has taken place since the 1960s, but one major factor may be that the nature of marriage itself has changed. Up until the 1960s marriage could be seen as a contract between husband and wife on their wedding day. Neither party can withdraw from a contract, unless it is violated by some offence:

I was a typical product of the 1950s and of my class. My parents inculcated an idea of duty into me. You don't divorce or separate for trivial reasons—if you're not getting on, or you're bored. Those aren't adequate reasons. Once you've said, 'I do' you jolly well do—unless an earthquake comes along and shakes you off your feet.

I believe, and my background always led me to believe, that one's word is one's bond and you do what you say you are going to do, and within a marriage that was even more important…

The traditional institution (man—breadwinner; woman—home-maker) has undergone a radical evolution in the second half of the twentieth century into a quest for personal and emotional fulfilment. It has become, ideally and theoretically, a developmental relationship of love. The need for 'fulfilment', and the expectation of it, places a heavy burden on what is now called the 'companionate' marriage. It is an axiom of human nature that where expectations run high disappointment can follow in equal ratio; where there is disappointment, disillusion; where disillusion, often bitterness and blame, and a constant suspicion that the grass may be greener elsewhere. Put simplistically, divorce happens when a relationship of need does not answer the expectations of one or both partners, and they cannot, or will not, remedy this to the satisfaction of both. The Divorce Reform Act of 1969 both reflected this evolution, and changed for ever—at a stroke—this understanding of the nature of marriage by making 'irretrievable breakdown' the only criterion for divorce. The implication was that it was the relationship between the spouses which conferred viability upon the union. A relationship, subject as it is to human failings and changes, can cease to exist, whereas a contract cannot.

If marriages fail more frequently it is because we are perhaps asking too much of them. The decade of the 'Self', the Sixties, introduced a paradox, for since then the natural human impulse to form a couple has clashed with a desire for what is now called 'self-actualization' as an autonomous individual.

The legacy of the Thatcher years

The 1980s and the early 1990s were more damaging in terms of emotional and psychological health than probably any Conservative politician will ever admit to. In the competitive, market-driven, 'on your bike' years there were inevitably more losers than winners, and the crushing effects on the individual of long-term unemployment, or of the exhaustion and stress of keeping afloat through the waves of slimming down, restructuring and short-term contracts, coincided with a period of mind-blowing technological change, but also with a downgrading of support and health services. Our daily environment became one of aggression, crime, hopelessness and failure. It is scarcely surprising that, along with all the other breakdowns, marriages crashed as well. The 'me' generation came up against a society which did not care for the individual, and as a result the structures which traditionally provided love, support and nurture started to crumble as never before.

One divorcee wrote of being alone in such a world:

For those with no loving partner, no family, no network of friends or community backing, alone and isolated, told to stand on their own two feet, sink or swim, fend for themselves, life is bleak indeed.

Nevertheless, stable and fulfilling unions do still happen, which raises the question of whether it is solely the concept of marriage that causes the problem, or whether there is a certain 'type' of person who is likely to divorce. There are indubitably people whose way of relating will not bring harmony to a relationship, and it is the combination of a dysfunctional relational system (usually learnt in early childhood) and the high hopes that marriage will satisfy their dreams which can often produce tension and ultimately termination.

The effects of divorce

Divorce is the great pandemic of our civilization, and in the wake of each broken marriage comes an engulfing wave of human misery. Becoming two separate individuals means tearing asunder more than just the relationship, and this is perhaps one of the most painful processes that can happen in adult life. Beyond the couple themselves are those whose lives may be touched, if not wrecked, by the storm. Prime among these are the children of the union, but the couple's parents also, may be deeply troubled and friends divided. Statistics suggest that remarriages (now around 40 per cent of all marriages) are more likely to finish than first ones—with what may now be several sets of children and stepchildren suffering. The State is involved: income supplements are often necessary; delinquency increases, health suffers. In some sectors of society, notably among those who account themselves religious, divorce can also still provoke scandal, stigma, censure, intolerance and ostracism.

There are other side-effects of a divorce. Analysis of statistics by One plus One[4], the Marriage and Partnership Research Charity, tells us that divorce is associated with higher relative risk of premature mortality and lower survival rates for cancers, and a higher rate of depression. Children of divorced parents are more susceptible to a range of health problems, and suffer more frequently from accidental injury, and nearly half non-custodial parents lose contact with their children within six years of the divorce.

It is estimated that:

- the cost of marital breakdown to a typical British business or organization through absenteeism and lost productivity is more than £5,000 per year for each divorcing individual;

- the public cost of divorce now stands at more than £4 billion a year.

In short, when a marriage collapses, it is not only the two individuals who bear the consequences, though theirs is the most immediate and acute suffering, but there is an impact on society as well. In this era of rapid change, this mass failure of marital relationships puts huge strain on the social structures.

It is a phenomenon with which society has to get to grips.

The Family Law Act 1996

The Family Law Act (which is examined in more detail in Appendix 1) was passed in the summer of 1996 and will come fully on stream during 1999. It attempts if not to halt this seemingly inexorable increase in broken homes, at least to palliate the consequences, by taking some of the adversarial and confrontational elements away, and also aims to limit the damage—primarily to children, but also to their divorcing parents. It prescribes a year's (or more, in certain cases) stepping back and reflecting before the decision to divorce can be made reality, and—by extending Legal Aid to family mediation—attempts to get the parties to decide amicably and fairly on the division of the household, its members and belongings.

Further clauses attempt to:

- remove the legal notion of 'fault' in matrimonial law;

- codify and strengthen existing legal remedies for the victims of domestic violence;

- provide measures to strengthen the protection of children's interests and welfare at all stages.

There will also be grants for the provision of marriage support services, research into the causes and ways of preventing marital breakdown.

The new Act was extensively researched, with much consultation of anyone who was anyone in the world of relationships, marital therapy and counselling, endlessly debated in press and Parliament, and amended, in the belief that—since the number of divorces each year doubled after the 'quickie' divorce came into effect in 1971—a slowing down of the procedure may consequently reduce the statistics... and possibly some of the misery.

It has yet to be proven. There is a school of thought among the professional marital counsellors and therapists that the new divorce legislation is psychologically unsound. A 'no conflict' divorce which aims to safeguard the interests of the children may not address all the feelings of injustice, incompleteness, rejection, unfairness and failure that the adults may suffer. While there are some couples who may just drift apart, and agree amicably on terms, mostly there is a bitter bloody dispute, which needs to be expressed and worked through.

What is this book about?

This book is about the feelings and consequences of the process of becoming 'I' instead of 'we'; two individuals instead of a couple, the slow disintegration of a common history. How do we let go of the man or woman with whom we promised to share our life for ever? of the person who is the co-parent of our children? How do we relinquish dreams and plans, security, shared memories? How do we mourn a relationship when half of it is alive and well and possibly living with a new partner on the other side of town? How does one flesh become two persons?

This dissolution may extend over many years, and our emotions will pass through several transitional stages as our circumstances change. In practical terms, however, the process usually has three distinct phases[5]:

- disengagement from the marriage—the period leading up to and immediately after the final breakup;

- intermediate phase—we understand the marriage is over, but have yet to grasp and adjust to the full implications;

■ the integration phase—the establishment of long-term patterns and routines within the new status.

This three-part process (which makes up the structure of this book) echoes the universal sequence of a rite of passage (the ceremonies which mark an individual's transition from one status to another within a given society)[6]:

■ separation—the old status is erased;

■ transition—stripped of all manifestations of his old role, the 'passenger' enters a suspended state between past and future identities;

■ reincorporation—the 'passenger' emerges from this threshold state and is reincorporated into society in his new role.

It also reflects the three stages of coming to terms with loss enumerated by the psychiatrist John Bowlby[7] in his seminal work on loss: protest, disorganization and reorganization.

The feelings experienced by the divorcee during these phases will fluctuate; for some the worst pain will be at the beginning, for others it may come much later as harsh reality bites. It is hard for us to take stock while on the emotional roller-coaster that is divorce; positive and negative succeed each other. Some people, especially those who had no warning of their partner's desire to divorce, may never fully adjust to their change in status.

The tripartite structure of this book reflects the roots, process, and the long-term effects of divorce. Although we shall briefly explore the questions of professional help for ailing marriages, social and religious factors, and (in Appendix 1) the new procedures under the 1996 legislation, the main focus is on the emotional process: the pain, the anger, the grieving, the bitterness, and the effect of all these on the health—emotional, psychological, physical—of the individuals concerned. Practical matters, finance and children will be included only in so far as they affect the negotiation of personal issues.

The resolution of these issues—the reasons for the breakdown of the relationship, guilt, failure, denial—influences how the man and woman emerge from the process of splitting up, and can be predictors of the success of any future relationship. Research and statistics suggest that men fare far worse from the divorce process than women do, and indeed it is a fact that more women than men file for divorce, especially in the earlier years of marriage. The difference between *his* divorce and *her* divorce in coming to terms with life alone will form one of the chapters of this book.

A significant proportion of this book will be given over to studying how divorced individuals go through the grieving process which follows any loss. But—as those who have been through it know—divorce as a bereavement is markedly different from that which follows a death. A marriage is a peculiarly fragile relationship, since the loss of one member destroys it. Yet it is a remarkably enduring social entity which is harder to destroy than to create:

Even when both members of a personal relationship act upon a mutual decision to terminate it, they may find the task of dismantling it beyond their capabilities.[8]

It involves a struggle not only through the darkness of pain but also through a range of negative emotions, often admixed with jealousy of the 'lost' spouse's new partner, and that hardest loss of all to bear, on which depends psychological survival: self-esteem. Many of those interviewed during the preparation of this book had been dealt what amounted to a mortal blow to their image of themselves as attractive, capable, normal, giving human beings. The tears that many shed as they spoke of their feelings were of a bitter regret for the people they once considered themselves to have been and felt they could not be again. All but a small handful of the divorced people who contributed to this book, and who had been left by their partners, were still struggling in one way or another to come to terms with what had happened. Most were still to some extent stuck in their own personal slough of despond and, despite therapy and counselling, family and new affairs, they were bitter, often lonely, and easily tearful. Most said they had rather their ex-partner had died.

Who is this book for?

This book is primarily for those caught up in the churning machinery of divorce. It is for those who are going through the process, for those considering it, and those recovering from it. It is for their family, their friends. I hope, too, it will be of help to all those concerned with the divorcing and the divorced—pastorally, socially, or in professional counselling situations.

Divorcing people often find it difficult both to identify their feelings and to work through them because they get completely overwhelmed by practical issues—children, finance, housing—and this book is therefore an attempt to help them stay with their emotions in a way that does not deal with the practical or the material. One man, divorced after three years because his wife went to live with another man, spoke for many when he said:

It's difficult at the time to process all the feelings.

This book is for those ground in the mill of divorce, that they may not feel isolated.

The positive side of divorce

I haven't found a good divorce yet. You can have an easy divorce, and counselling can help. You can be civilized but no… not a good divorce.
COUNSELLOR

I do think it is possible for two people to realize they don't have a viable marriage but yet to give their children a model of friendship.

THERAPIST

If divorce is a life sentence, it does not have to be a prison. Although this book inevitably focuses on the negative, it also highlights the positive factors which may emerge. It is about the process of coming out of pain, out of the anguish which is the common thread through all the stories of separation and ending, and moving on, either as a single person or into a new partnership. To do this we must confront reality and accept the situation; we must ask ourselves hard questions about our contribution to the breakdown; about whether we wish to change, and how we shall find the strength and support to do so. It is easier to project the blame for failure on to the other person, and get rid of our self-loathing in anger towards our 'ex', but this means we shall remain for ever in a cut-off world of dishonesty, which effectively prevents any real interrelation with other people, and will certainly quickly mar a new intimate relationship. We must confront our anger and pain, and turn these into positive energy; face our fear of change and of the unknown.

Forgiveness

When we can do all this we shall be a very long way towards understanding the key to letting go (not only of the relationship, but also of the relational system that we learned young) and to moving forward. Another vital key factor in moving on is forgiveness. To many reading this, this may seem an impossibility at present, when wounds are too raw, and injustice burns within us like acid. But it is possible, and this book is about the process of getting there.

What this book is not

We have already said that this is not a book which focuses on practical issues and consequences except in so far as these affect the feelings of those going through the process, or as they themselves are in turn affected by emotional factors. Many will ask how it is possible to write a book on the pain of divorce without a chapter on the suffering of the children of the marriage. This book is solely about the (former) partners of the marriage, and what they will go through. Of course the question of our children will have an enormous bearing on what we feel and do, but the book is not in itself about the children. There are many works on the shelves which deal with their agony.[9]

It is not a book which guides the reader through the steps of legal consultation, nor does it give any help whatsoever on finance or any practical matter. Again, this is readily available in the many 'how to' handbooks on the market.

Illustrative material for this book came from a variety of sources. Primarily it came from interviews with divorced people themselves, and secondarily from individual marriage and relationship counsellors, mainly from the two organizations Relate and Marriage Care. In all cases names have been omitted or changed (except in the case of one woman, who wished to be identified as the author of the stories and poems inspired by her divorce. These stood for what so many others have experienced, and have been used with her permission.) Some circumstantial detail has been altered sufficiently to safeguard confidentiality without distorting cases. Another source of background material for this book has been articles and reports in newspapers and magazines published primarily during the 1990s. If fascination with divorce reflects the current trend, it also suggests the converse—that marriage, its problems and difficulties, are still of intense interest.

I use the term 'divorcee' to apply to both men and women. In order to avoid the use of non-inclusive language and the clumsiness of saying 'him/her' all the time, I have used the inclusive plural pronoun and adjective throughout, though some readers may be uncomfortable with this as grammatically incorrect. I have also frequently used the first person plural (we/us/our) when talking of situations and emotions with which many will identify.

Divorce by and large is hell. One matrimonial solicitor[10] said:

> In reality, however bad you think the whole divorce will be, it is likely to be worse than anticipated.

For those who know, or who are about to enter this reality, it may help to know that even though the effects of divorce will stay with them, the process need not destroy them, and that in life it is often pain rather than complacency that can be the springboard for change and growth.

1. Nicky Hart, *When Marriage Ends. A Study in Status Passage*, Tavistock Publications, 1976.
2. Ronald L. Simons and Associates, *Understanding Differences Between Divorced and Intact Families—Stress, Interaction, and Child Outcome*, Sage Publications, 1996.
3. John Morgan, *Debrett's New Guide to Etiquette and Modern Manners*, Headline, 1996.
4. *Marital Breakdown and the Health of the Nation*, ed. Fiona McAllister, One plus One, 1995 (second edition).
5. From 'Contrasts and correspondences in the meaning of marital breakdown for men and women', a paper given by Nicky Hart to the 1974 Conference of the British Sociological Society on Sexual Divisions and Society.
6. Arnold van Gennep, *Les Rites de Passage (The Rites of Passage)*, E. Nourry, Paris 1907, and Routledge and Kegan Paul, London.
7. John Bowlby, *Attachment and Loss: volume 3: Loss, sadness and depression*, Penguin, 1991. © The Tavistock Institute of Human relations, 1980
8. George J. McCall in *Personal Relationships 4: dissolving personal relationship*, ed. S. Duck, Academic Press, 1982.
9. See 'Further Reading' list page 231–32
10. Simone Katzenburg, *The Seven Stages of Divorce*, Solomon Taylor and Shaw, 1996.

PART 1:

The breakdown of a marriage

Introduction

> To live is to act and to cease, to wait and to rest, and then begin acting again, but in a different way.[1]

Because our lives are constantly moving forward, so too are our relationships, and marriage is also a dynamic process. As we change during our lifetime, our partner's perception of us will change as well, sometimes to such a degree that they will feel betrayed and hurt. 'You're not the person I married any longer!' is the cry of a wounded human being who thinks their spouse has reneged on the original deal—something which can result in bitterness and rows.

Divorce can happen at any point in this process, though there are flashpoints and periods when breakup is more likely. Before we investigate the signs which warn of marital problems, it is useful to understand how a marriage, or any intimate relationship, develops through time. The sequence and main characteristics of the developmental stages of marriage are these[2]:

The Stages of marriage

Romance

This is the honeymoon period when we are blissfully in love. We see only our partner's positive points, and in this unconditional acceptance and exclusive intimacy, we shut ourselves off from the world in a glow of intense emotion through which we view every experience. Sometimes we are more in love with being in love than with our partner. We need

24

and give plentiful nurturing during this stage, which mirrors the first months of a baby's life when mother and child spend hours physically close in a warm symbiotic oneness, and when mother provides every need. During this stage of a relationship the foundations are laid for mutual caring, support and trust.

Reality

As the reality of living with another human being breaks in, and we discover some of the 'downside' of our partner, it is rare that this first ecstasy of closeness lasts. Aspects of the other emerge which can displease or irritate us, and if our expectations of total fulfilment, passion, and happiness ever after were high, then the crash of disappointment will be correspondingly loud as our hopes tumble around us. It is at this stage that many 'young' marriages falter, and if the couple do not learn how to communicate their feelings accurately and to negotiate difficulties then divorce may follow swiftly. As we saw earlier (see page 11) 10 per cent of marriages break up within two years, and one in nine divorce within five. Adapting to the harsh reality of marriage may be all the more difficult since it is often at this stage that babies come along, with all the mess and stress that they inevitably bring. Anger and depression escalate, and the curve of marital satisfaction flattens out abruptly.

Power struggles

The struggle to be our own person while being in a couple, to regain the independence, or—as it may be seen—liberty of carefree bachelor days is at its height during the post-romance days in a marriage. One or both partners may be seeking out new directions. If one is left behind they may feel threatened or abandoned. The issue of 'Who decides for me? for us?' can flavour every exchange, and an emotional chasm may open up between them which will be hard to bridge without true communication, and this can be a time of violent rows or chilly distancing.

Finding ourselves

Although the average length of a marriage in the United Kingdom is now fewer than ten years, a quarter of all divorces occur between the sixteenth and twenty-fifth years. This is the time of the 'empty nesters', when children are growing up and going, and the couple discover that parenting was the glue that held them together. There is more time to pay attention to personal needs and wants, and both men and women may discover an emotional vacuum which demands to be filled— either with a new career, different preoccupations, or maybe a new relationship to add some zest to the onset of middle age. We know our partners so well by now, and we may become bored unless the marriage has been kept fresh and alive. Menopause and 'mid-life crisis', redundancy or early retirement, and the death of our own parents, may all be factors which can trigger a change of direction and lead to divorce.

Working through

Fewer divorces occur after the Silver Wedding anniversary, for couples who have made it this far will be less concerned about themselves, more settled and secure and thus more able to give. Flexibility and negotiation will be more practised skills, and the couple will be able to appreciate the plus points of being without children. Nevertheless, there are factors which may cause husband and wife to have to go back and rework an earlier stage of their marital development. The retirement of one partner, for example, when the other has been used to space and liberty at home may come hard, or it might be that the presence of a parent or in-law brings almost intolerable strains on a previously smooth relationship.

Andrea and Kenneth

Andrea's husband Kenneth had taken early retirement. Andrea found herself increasingly stressed out of all proportion to the domestic irritation caused by her husband's presence, and would—uncharacteristically—rage at her husband, with whom she normally had a placid and satisfying relationship. Things became so strained that they sought counselling. It emerged that Andrea had been five when her father came home from the War, and she had deeply resented the arrival of this 'stranger'. With Kenneth at home these early feelings had come flooding back.

If these and other points of conflict cannot be negotiated satisfactorily, then divorce can still happen, as it may—even late in life—if the degradation of the relationship extends over a long period. This was said by a man divorced after nearly forty years of marriage:

For the last ten years the marriage might have been on the slippery slope, but there was no talk of divorce. There was not a lot of communication, but I still believe it could have been saved if somebody had taken us and banged our heads together.

Collaboration

It is rare to see a couple divorcing in this, the stage of evolution of relationship where we fully accept our partner and are fully accepted in return. Both husband and wife feel secure in this acceptance, and are thus free to grow and explore new ways of fulfilment without being any threat to the other. Old age does, however, bring upheavals and traumas to be met—bereavement, illness, diminishing strength, moving to different accommodation—and these may require couples to return again and work through previous stages of their development as a couple. If they do not, results can be disastrous. Leo Tolstoy, in his eighties, left his wife of forty or so years, who had borne him thirteen children, determined to sever the ties of matrimony. Matrimony, however, did not let go of him so easily; he died a few days later of a chill which turned to pneumonia at Astapova Station.

There is usually no one moment when a couple know their marriage is dead, finished. Dr Jack Dominian, founder of the marriage and partnership research organization One plus One, said:

There is usually a deterioration, and one or other grasps experientially the gap between how they want the relationship to be and how it is. This could be the result of an affair, or talking to friends, for example. You know things are not OK, and once you perceive the gap between dream and reality the process begins. If you push your spouse towards your dream, and they are unable to fulfil it, then disenchantment grows, and quarrels become frequent rows, communication falters and stops. These are the death knells of relationship.

The factors that push you to divorce are pain—each person has their own pain threshold in a relationship—and apathy and indifference, when your partner means nothing to you.

This first part of the book is about the lead-up to the decision to divorce, and lists some of the signs which warn that a marriage may be on the rocks. It then explores the possibility of saving the marriage, of seeking professional help, and of separation—which may be enforced if one partner walks out, or an agreed and structured trial time of being apart. Finally we look at the decision, however it is made, to dissolve the formal bond of marriage by divorce.

1. Arnold van Gennep, *Les Rites de Passage (The Rites of Passage)*, E. Nourry, Paris, 1907, and Routledge and Kegan Paul, London.
2. These developmental stages were first formulated in the work of Liberty Kovaks of the Center for Marriage and Family Therapy, Sacramento CA, who has made her work available to the author, and then by Deirdre Morrod of One plus One. They were expanded by the author in *The Marriage Work-Out Book*, Lion Publishing, 1996.

1

The beginning of the end?

1. The marriage has been deteriorating because of the Respondent's behaviour for a considerable number of years.

2. In 1993 the Respondent indicated that he no longer wished to go on holiday with the Petitioner and since then they have taken separate holidays.

3. The Petitioner has felt that she has been treated as a housekeeper for the last fifteen years of the marriage. The Respondent has a number of irritating habits, e.g. he has written the date in dust to emphasize to the Petitioner that she has not dusted, and has criticized her severely for this.

4. The Respondent is very argumentative and there is no companionship between the parties. The Respondent cannot discuss anything without an argument developing. This is particularly embarrassing for the Petitioner when this occurs in front of friends.

5. The Respondent is extremely unreasonable in his attitude towards the Petitioner, e.g. he told the Petitioner that if she took care of a close friend's pet while they were on holiday, he would leave her. This would not have inconvenienced him in any way.

6. For a number of years the Respondent has threatened to leave. The Petitioner now feels that the stress of her marital difficulties is affecting her health, and that the marriage is at an end.

Thus a solicitor's letter sounded the death knell of a marriage which had lasted half a lifetime: a human tragedy expressed in the language of farce; the highest human bond reduced to a squabble over a dusty scribble.

For the respondent in question above, divorce arrived out of an apparently cloudless sky. Another man, Stuart, married twenty-seven years, came home from work one day to find his wife missing. After he had rung the police, his grown-up daughter telephoned to say that her mother had gone to stay with her parents and was not coming home. And she didn't. Stuart had picked up no clue that she was unhappy. Dan, in his fifties, also came home from the office, said starkly 'I'm leaving you', and went to live with another woman.

These shock stories of brutal breakings of the bond abound, and are particularly common in divorces occurring after fifteen years of marriage.

But no marriage breakdown ever really happens out of the blue at whatever stage. It may be a case of anger so intense that there is no doubt of the outcome, or a growing absence of communication over the years, a slow but sure emotional disengagement. Sometimes there has never been emotional engagement. People continue together out of habit, necessity or fear, without realizing how affectively, or emotionally, stuck they are. They marry, earn money, buy a home, furnish it, have children, remain with their partner. One counsellor said:

Acquiring status symbols is seen as 'working together'. It's amazing how often fitted carpets figure in couple counselling! But one day one of them wakes up, and it is more often the wife, and realizes they are emotionally starved.

Marriages can die emotionally through either famine or war, or it may be that they have never truly lived. A non-existent or moribund relationship can be tolerated for a time, smoothed over, ignored, but eventually matters come to a head, and this moment is reached sooner or later according to how high the expectations of the marriage are—or maybe how strong a sense of duty one has:

> *I was a morally vacuous young man, but one did one's duty as a matter of habit. You went down tramlines, and because the tramlines were there you didn't have to think. I wasn't a moral agent in a conscious, witting way.*

For those who have grown up to expect an emotionally rich idyll of love the realization may be rapid; for older generations discovery of one's self with its unfulfilled needs and desires may take longer:

> *I was thrashing about trying to find out who the f*** I was. I was donning and doffing roles to see if they'd fit.*

It may not take place till children have grown up and there is liberty to attend to personal issues.

Warning signs

Life changes

Major life changes can often contribute to the breakdown of a marriage:

- small children
- the 'empty nest'
- elderly relatives living in the marital home
- the death of parents
- major illness
- changes in professional life

Not only each partner but also the relationship must adapt to changes. If it does not then it may crumble and die.

Lack of communication

She kept saying 'Speak to me, speak to me,' while we were making love. What did she want me to say, for heaven's sake, 'Er... the stock market's looking good'?

Carla, aged thirty-five, married for thirteen years and with two children, says her marriage has never been a good one, and blames it on her husband's inability to communicate:

I can't feel his love and I don't believe it exists. He never talks about issues, about us. I think he just wants a home and family and all that those provide, but I don't feel we are in a partnership, working together. We just happen to live together and be parents of the same children, but we're parallel rather than together. We're in a loveless marriage and he must accept that there's no point in going on and four people being miserable.

A relationship without communication is like a brain starved of oxygen: there will be irreparable damage and it will die—or continue in a lifeless shell, brain-dead, persistently vegetative, sustained artificially from habit, or 'for the sake of the children'. Couples must either make the commitment to learn how to communicate effectively, or they may disconnect permanently:

I couldn't converse with her one-to-one. I'd end up talking to the wall. I didn't want her to agree with everything—I wanted dialogue.

There was not a lot of communication, perhaps because of my hearing. But I got such enjoyment and relaxation from my gardening that I probably spent more time than I should have in the garden.

Communication is not simply a matter of saying, 'Your dinner's in the oven, dear,' or, 'I'm going to be late home tonight,' or even, 'The stock market's looking good.' True communication means being and imparting our real selves, but that implies a knowledge and acceptance of ourselves, and not everyone is secure enough, or sufficiently aware of their own feelings and emotions, to be able to do this. Communication is a skill which is learned, ideally in our family of origin. It is not innate. When we can express genuinely both the positive and the negative—our love, warmth, tenderness, concern, admiration, and our anger, jealousy, irritation, fear or grief, and their causes, we 'own' these emotions as ours. We communicate them because they belong to us; our partner is not the cause of them.

In many marriage breakdowns communication is replaced by blaming the other, by recrimination and accusation:

■ You never pick up your dirty clothes and put them in the bin. You expect me to act as your mother, and you make me sick!

■ You're a selfish pig and you're always late and you make me angry. I hate you!

■ Look, you've made me cross again.

■ You make me so tired, all this talk, talk, talk…

Sexual communication

Between husband and wife sexual intimacy and (usually) intercourse are powerful indicators of the state of their overall relationship. These are prime means of communication of feelings—of love, affection, joy, comfort and security but also of forgiveness, healing and reconciliation. Sex—or lack of it—can speak out the things we sometimes cannot or dare not say:

We'd had no sexual relationship since the children had left home. It had gone cold. I had done my duty.

She would go off sex for two to three months at a time, and there was a nagging worry about this. She wouldn't talk about it in front of anyone.

There was always a price to pay and eventually she decided it was an 'invasion of her privacy' and gave it up altogether.

There are inevitably times in the course of a marriage when sexual activity is likely to wane: during pregnancy and after childbirth, at times of intense stress, fatigue and illness. There may be other medical reasons which preclude intercourse. But couples in love can always cuddle and touch, stroke and caress, give comfort and solace as well as pleasure. Separate rooms can often signal a relationship which has gone astray somewhere, the physical wall symbolizing the emotional barrier. In general terms the couple's sexual relationship is a microcosm of the whole relationship, of their ability to communicate, to be unselfish, to give and to please.

In some warring couples sexuality can be used as a weapon: withdrawal of one's availability to one's partner, or the forcing of unreasonable demands on them suggests loathing or contempt (often one's own feelings about oneself projected on to the partner):

He was extremely sexually active, which I found a great burden. In the end he asked me to go to bed with [other] people, which I did—with men and women. I agreed to that because I felt I was failing him in some way. But in all honesty, apart from a little problem at the beginning of our marriage, I never failed to have a climax, and nor did he.

Sexually… at some stage in the last ten years of our marriage…

he made it clear to me that he had to have anal intercourse, and there was the underlying implication that if I wouldn't do that he'd leave me, so I started to engage in that, and I really did find that…

'*The Respondent shows the petitioner no natural love and affection. The Petitioner and Respondent have not had sexual relations since 1980. The Respondent initially made excuses, e.g. saying that he was tired. The Petitioner always hoped that matters would improve, that the Respondent would show some physical affection, but this did not happen. The Respondent would not discuss the problems.*'

EXTRACT FROM SOLICITOR'S LETTER

The sexual relationship between two partners almost invariably mirrors the wider relationship, and the respect, esteem and love the one feels for the other.

Infidelity

An affair is often the trigger for divorce, but although it plays a part in approximately one-third of marriage breakdowns, it is seldom the underlying cause. Rarely, too, is an extra-marital relationship prompted solely by a need for *sexual* experience unavailable at home. It is usually a symptom of what is going on, or not going on, within the marriage itself, and can be seen as an acting out of something unresolved in the marriage, or of something missing. This might be merely fun and the thrill of 'living dangerously', or may be a more serious, but unconscious, search for a fulfilment which has never been present from early childhood onwards, and which it was hoped marriage would provide. Passion allures, beckons, and can dominate and override when life is otherwise routine and flavourless. Adultery often signals a crisis point in the marriage which can lead either to a reconstruction of the relationship, or ultimately to disintegration.

James and Michelle

James had been married to Michelle for twenty-four years, and they had both been faithful throughout that time. However, the relationship was strained to breaking-point by Michelle's drinking, which resulted in tense or embarrassing incidents privately and publicly, and by James' emotional immaturity, which made him selfish and in quest of perpetual mothering. Both came from devout Catholic families, which were joined in marriage by other family members, and neither had been out with anyone else before marriage. Both worked in church-linked 'caring' organizations in a medium-sized town, and had respected public roles. The pressure to remain within the marriage and toe the party (Church) line on marriage was intense. James, aged forty-nine, started a passionate sexual affair with a French woman, thus kicking over the traces of his conventional life. The affair lasted only fifteen months, but was discovered within weeks of its start by Michelle, since James had 'accidentally-on-purpose' left evidence visible at home. This effectively removed him from a marriage which should probably never have existed. Eventually, after much agonizing, he and Michelle started divorce proceedings.

In James' case, infidelity was the breaking of a taboo, and his French lover, Marie, became for him the 'transitional emotional object' that helped him to leave the marriage. Without this overriding passion he could not have let go of the marriage, despite the hell he endured conjugally. Marie to him fulfilled the same role as the teddy bear or the blanket which give solace, enabling children to spend time away from mother.

Various needs within the marriage may spark a sexual relationship outside it. So often the grass can indeed be greener on the other side, for moribund marriages can be cold, joyless, distant and grim, or unpleasant, angry, bitter and violent. The person who symbolizes freedom, warmth, understanding, intimacy, excitement and love—and who does not nag or represent routine—can hold out the hope of a fresh start, and by implication a goodbye to all the problems of life:

> *I feel different when I'm with her; she understands me and I feel more alive when I'm with her. All I get at home is rows, rows, rows and we always spend the weekend shopping.*
>
> 52-YEAR-OLD MAN OF HIS 26-YEAR-OLD MISTRESS

Among the younger-married, too, infidelity is becoming more current. According to Annette Lawson in her study *Adultery*[1], women married before 1960 who had an affair started it after, on average, fourteen years of marriage. Between 1960 and 1969 the timing was down to eight years, and after 1970 the extra-marital relationship got going after an average of four years. This may be explained by the rising expectations of emotional fulfilment with which women in particular enter marriage, and of sexual enjoyment for men.

There may be many other explanations for looking outside the marriage for what is not perceived to be there: people need affirmation and self-esteem, wanting their importance as human beings to be mirrored, if only transitorily, in the eyes of their lover; they crave sexual gratification and excitement; they want to 'find themselves' as people; they seek to punish the spouse; they seek relief from boredom. In almost all cases the romance and fantasy created with a new partner mask the issues which are unresolved in the marriage, and which will, inevitably, recreate similar situations in a new relationship.

Rupert and Linda

Rupert, a high-flying and successful businessman, had been twice married and divorced, both times after affairs with women at work. He came to couple therapy with his new wife, Linda, whom he had also met in the office, because Linda had discovered that Rupert was being unfaithful to her—and again with a woman from work. Rupert now was keen to discover what drove him to keep repeating his destructive behaviour patterns (he was able to deny and 'forget' previous relationships), and to make sense of his life. Divorce, which is on the cards, will not solve anything for Rupert, and he must come to understand what unfulfilled need he is seeking to complete in his serial relationships.

There are, of course, times when a fleeting infidelity—an encounter while away from home, a moment of inebriated lechery at an office party, an afternoon of housebound loneliness and depression—may never be confessed, and perhaps quickly forgotten; or—if admitted—forgiven. Sometimes husband and wife will both stray from time to time, but the marriage will hold good.

But for all the permissiveness and 'openness' of marriage in Anglo-Saxon countries at the dawn of the twenty-first century, infidelity, if discovered, hurts the faithful spouse, and damages the relationship:

I couldn't stand the lies. When you're constantly lied to it does something to your brain. You start to doubt your sanity because your guts are telling you one thing, and your partner is telling you another thing, and you want what he says to be true. It does something to your trust in other people, and it's very, very painful... Two years later he started it again, and he recycled the same old things. There was a crunch moment when I was fetching my aunt from Wales and he was supposed to be in the house, but he wasn't. He wasn't where he said he was, and I just had to face the doubt.

The pain and mistrust it causes can ultimately destroy the marriage, for it is not only a betrayal but it suggests strongly that all has not been well underneath the surface, and that there has been dissatisfaction for some time. It can be a devastating blow from which the marriage—and the other spouse—may not recover. One partner's world of passionate fantasy may suddenly become a reality of agonizing choice for both, and enduring pain for the deserted one. Furthermore, those who remarry after a divorce caused by their partner's infidelity take that mistrust, anger and fear into any future relationship with them.

Although men have more affairs than women[2], they find it harder to forgive adultery on the part of their wives, and are more likely to petition for divorce because of it, than women are over male infidelity.[3]

Conflict

Conflict is not inevitably the sign of a disintegrating marriage, but if prolonged and repeated, with no evolution of the process of arguing, it can herald the breakdown of a loving relationship. Everyone argues, and a marriage which does not feel the pinch of a quarrel from time to time is emotionally dead. It is *how* couples disagree and resolve their differences that often gives a clue as to whether their marriage will grow and mature, or whether the pain of blocked communication, frustration, incompatibility and sometimes violence—verbal or physical— will grow too great to be borne:

> *'Meaningful' rows when you talk things out are OK, but the repetitive 'You did,' 'I didn't,' is futile, and brings disintegration.*
>
> JACK DOMINIAN [4]

The behaviour of the individual is often determined by the manner in which their own family of origin (and back through the generations) handled conflict. We learn our system of interacting from our earliest days, and it is hard to let go of it when we make our own intimate relationships in adult life. It is, however, possible to unlearn this system of interacting before the damage we do to our partner, our marriage and ultimately ourself is irreparable.

Conflict becomes terminal usually when it is a persistent element of interaction between the couple. The emotional maturity of the two individuals may determine its course: for instance the person who has never grown beyond an early stage of emotional development may scream, shout or cry during conflict, or act like a thwarted toddler, even lashing out physically. The one who has never moved beyond the stage of 'who decides?' (which Freud called the 'anal stage'), will make every small domestic issue a power struggle. But if we can trust our partner sufficiently with our emotions, conflict can actually help the relationship grow, by improving our skills of communication and negotiation and the process of problem solving.

Conversely, when there is not a good basis of trust, if communication at more than a superficial level is absent, if the partners do not feel secure, if they employ coercion, confrontation, self-justification or denial, if they use defence mechanisms to hide their real selves and feelings, if they are concerned only for themselves and their identity and self-image, if there is violence of any sort, then conflict will cause on-going unhappiness which the couple may be powerless to resolve without help, and the relationship may gradually dissolve.

Each unhappy family is, as Tolstoy observed in *Anna Karenina*, unhappy in its own way, but there are problem situations common to most marriages, and the most frequent subjects for rows are:

- jealousy—time given by one partner to third parties;

- demonstration of affection, feelings of rejection, criticism;

- finance—paying bills, overspending, areas of personal expenditure;

- sex—timing, frequency, manner of intercourse, physical affection;

- communication—not listening, not responding, not making one's inner world available to the partner;

- in-laws—time spent with, visits, interference;

- household responsibilities—chores, maintenance, shopping, management of children, roles;

- personal habits.

One other area which is now common, is the subject of a prior marriage or relationship, for those in second marriages:

Jancis is not happy about any contact I have with Charlotte. She feels very threatened by it.

Dysfunctional couples who argue, who snipe and bitch constantly, will choose, usually unconsciously, one of their habitual topics to 'go on about' and let it carry the weight, if not the venom, of all their dissatisfaction and unhappiness.

Violence

Sometimes unresolved conflict—aided by sheer frustration and desperation, consumption of alcohol, or being inured to it in one's early years—will escalate into violence. This may be physical (the 'domestic', dreaded by police called out to fights between husband and wife), sexual, emotional or mental.

She would hit, snatch, kick, grab. We were both verbally hostile. I don't know how I didn't murder her at the end. I'm glad I didn't.

She would hit me and throw things.

On one or two occasions he did push me about, but he never actually caused bruising. He would take his anger out on things though it was directed at me. Then there was an almighty row. It concerned my children, and there was a lot of violence, and I felt that really was the bottom line; there was no coming back after that. He left and this time it was so bad I felt it was not my place to ring up and say, 'Please come back'. So I just left it.

I threw a mirror at him which shattered, and I threw a bowl of water over him, and a couple of glasses of wine at various stages in the last few months of our marriage, because it didn't matter what I said, how I tried to explain how I felt, he didn't seem to take anything in.

It will often be the case that if one partner suffers from low self-esteem they will often unconsciously seek a controlling, dominant partner. Low self-esteem also causes people to put up with violent or abusive treatment:

It's the low self-esteem thing, that's why I started to engage in anal intercourse when he wanted it.

Analyses of grounds for divorce do not single out violence as a cause. It comes under the blanket of 'unreasonable behaviour', which covers a multitude of sins. In 1993 22.6 per cent of petitions for divorce from men were on the grounds of unreasonable behaviour, and 55.6 per cent of those from women.[5]

Predicting divorce

Research done in the United States by Professor Howard Markman[6] of the University of Denver hit the headlines in the British press in the autumn of 1996, when he told a conference that *how* we argue is a more reliable predictor of the prospects of an enduring marriage than the subject matter of the dispute. Markman and his team spent twenty years following couples through from courtship, mapping their progress, and now claim that they can predict 90 per cent of divorces. Marriages are most at risk when partners walk away from arguments or let little points escalate into major disputes. On the other hand, appeasement, says Markman, rarely works, for it leads to pursuit. The wife, frustrated in her attempt to get her husband to rise to her bait, complains longer and louder: 'If you are not being heard,' says Markman, 'You turn the volume up.' Escalation is another danger sign. Markman says:

> 'You start off disagreeing about how to put the soap in the dishwasher and wind up talking about leaving.'

Research[7] into the physiological processes at work when conflict escalates suggests that men feel more bodily arousal and pain during conflict with their spouse, and thus tend to withdraw from argument by 'stonewalling'—avoiding eye contact, holding the neck and facial muscles rigid. When this happens, communication ceases, and the possibility of any satisfactory outcome recedes rapidly. The man, overwhelmed by the woman's emotions, seeks avoidance, and follows his physical withdrawal by an emotional one. She responds by advancing as he withdraws, trying to re-engage him, which sets up a crescendoing pattern of anger, frustration and mutual misery.

But at least there is some hope at this stage. If the couple are not helped out of their repetitive conflictual sequences, it is usually the woman who then withdraws emotionally in disgust, and the lives of the two people who once may have experienced their relationship as a paradisiac garden become distant and parallel courses. When this happens the marriage is on its way to separation and divorce.

Is your marriage heading for divorce? Some questions to ask about your relationship[8]

Answer these questions by yourself (not with your partner), using the following three-point scale to rate how often you and your partner experience these:

Write 1, 2, or 3 in the boxes as appropriate:
1 = rarely
2 = sometimes
3 = frequently

❏ Little arguments escalate into ugly fights with accusations, criticisms, name-calling, or bringing up past hurts.

❏ My partner criticizes or belittles my feelings, opinions, or desires.

❏ My partner seems to view my words or actions more negatively than I mean them to be.

❏ When we have a problem to solve it is as if we are in opposite teams.

❏ I hold back from telling my partner what I really think and feel.

❏ I think seriously about what it would be like to date or marry someone else.

❏ I feel lonely in this relationship.

❏ When we argue, one of us withdraws… that is, doesn't want to talk about it any more, or leaves the scene.

Who tends to withdraw more when there is an argument?

■ Male

- Female

- Both equally

- Neither

These questions were based on fifteen years of research on the kinds of communication and conflict management patterns that predict if a relationship is headed for trouble. The higher the score the greater danger your relationship is in, unless changes are made.

- 8–12 Green light

Your relationship is good at this time, but in the next year you could have a stronger relationship. Any relationship can head in the opposite direction if you don't work at it.

- 13–17 Yellow light

You need to be cautious—there are warning signs of patterns that should not be allowed to get worse. Take action to protect and improve what you have; spend time strengthening your relationship.

- 18–24 Red light

Stop and think about where the two of you are heading. There are patterns present that could put your relationship at significant risk.

1. Annette Lawson, *Adultery*, Blackwell, Oxford, 1988.
2. A. Johnson, J.Wadworth, K. Wellings and J. Field, *Sexual Attitudes and Lifestyles*, Blackwell Scientific Publications, 1994.
3. Lord Chancellor's department *Looking to the Future: mediation and the ground for divorce*, HMSO, 1993.
4. Jack Dominian in an interview with the author, 1996.
5. Lord Chancellor's department *(see above)*.
6. Professor Howard Markman, material presented to a conference organised by One plus One, London, 22 October 1996, also H.J. Markman, S.M. Stanley, & S.L. Blumberg, *Fighting for your Marriage: Positive steps for a loving and lasting relationship*, Jossey Bass inc., San Francisco, 1994.
7. J.M. Gottman, *Marital Interactions: Experimental Investigations*, Academic Press, New York, 1979.
8. Professor Howard Markman, *(see above)*.

2

Can a marriage be saved?

My advice would be talk to a counsellor who can help you communicate your differences to each other to find ways of making the relationship more mutually satisfying. I do think our relationship could have been saved. Relate opened the eyes of both of us, but by that time it was too late.

If the warning signs of impending conjugal disaster go unheeded, if conflict is ignored, if we refuse to deal with it and allow it to go unresolved or persist in using it destructively, then our marriage will inevitably be seriously damaged. Again, if we take no notice of the growing wall of silence or bitterness between us, or if we try to solve problems alone, or 'pretend' something never happened, if we sacrifice ourselves and soldier on for the sake of an illusory peace, then these warning signs will increase, manifest themselves insistently and lead to a serious crisis.

Many will experience a time of ambiguity and uncertainty, when life together may seem intolerable. Resentment and anger will constantly well up; communication may be at an all-time low, and each exchange will be newly bruising and painful, picking open old scabs, inflicting fresh wounds.

Or it may be that, as we saw in the previous chapter, there are husbands and wives who are taken by surprise, to whom the departure of their spouse, or the request for a divorce, comes as a devastating shock, for they have seen no threatening clouds on the horizon:

She announced to me that she wanted to leave three weeks before she actually did, I didn't know how to handle the situation... I had no idea she was so unhappy that she wanted to leave the marriage.

When, in one way or another, the realization dawns that the marriage is in deep trouble, the couple may step back, for a variety of reasons (they may have children; the emotional or indeed financial investment in their life together may be too great; there may be social, family or religious pressures to stay together; there may be years of habit which are hard to break), and decide they must save the relationship.

Can the wounds of infidelity be healed?

A marriage can survive an affair and become stronger as a result, but it takes more than a willingness to forgive and forget once the confession is made or the adultery discovered. It is not a question of patching together the bits and pieces and hoping to remake a serviceable model. Rebuilding a relationship requires an honest and often painful examination not only of the marriage before the affair, but of the unresolved problems of childhood that hinder the sustaining of intimate relationship. It will usually be found that one or other partner had expressed dissatisfaction to some extent, and had gone unheard and unheeded, or that both had been dissatisfied in a number of ways.

'How would anybody react in a situation like that?' he says. 'Of course I was angry and felt betrayed... I wanted to sit down and talk things through. But there was no attempt on her part to patch things up.'

BARBIE DUTTER, 'TWO SIDES OF A FAILED MARRIAGE', THE *DAILY TELEGRAPH*,

29 AUGUST 1997

If the trust that once existed between the two cannot be rebuilt it is unlikely that the relationship can be either, and the vital romance and enjoyment of the early days of their love, which are necessary for starting anew, will not be rediscovered. The 'erring' partner must make a commitment never to see the third party, and to remain faithful. Sometimes the pain of this choice is too much, and they simply cannot give up the thrill and passion of the new relationship:

> It was unbearable. I felt compelled like an addict, unable to back off, despite the fact that Barbara [his wife] and I got on better in terms of harmoniousness than Yvonne and I.

Even if both partners are determined to try again, there will nevertheless be considerable tension between them, and flare-ups will be likely.

Professional help

For them, and for any couple who have reached crisis point, and cannot negotiate under this stress because of the high level of conflict, or sheer indifference, and who want to know whether it is possible to make a go of their relationship or whether they would be better to part as cleanly as possible, counselling or couple therapy may help them see more clearly their way ahead and enable them to follow it:

> Have they really thought it through? Sometimes they see it as an opening to freedom, a wonderful new social life et cetera, but when the harsh reality (of divorce) comes they see it's not as they thought. They have to be sure of all of their facts before. Organizations such as Relate or Marriage Care can help by enabling the decision-making process. But until you've tried it you don't really know.
>
> RELATE COUNSELLOR

It is important when seeking professional help in a relational crisis to find out whether the counsellor (or the organization to which the counsellor is affiliated) considers the individual or the relationship to be the client. Often when only one half of the couple seeks help, this results in personal development, growth, in finding one's own identity, and this can exacerbate an already disintegrating situation. And if one partner is dragged unwillingly to counselling, resentment and entrenchment can result:

> *The slope was getting quite slippery, Betty went to Relate. I went along with her. Well, it was all her pluses and my minuses. The thing that stopped me in my tracks was the counsellor. She must have been about twenty-three—it was just like being with my own daughter.*

A couple counsellor will not attempt to save the marriage at all costs, and will rather attempt to enable the couple to take responsibility for the decision they ultimately take to continue or end the marriage. Counselling helps people by providing them with a secure base when all else may be crumbling, and a safe and reliable relationship (with the counsellor) in which they can explore the situation, express all their feelings and gain greater insight that will help them deal more effectively with their lives. Self-esteem, which takes such a battering during marital problems and divorce, can be boosted to a level which keeps depression at bay and makes effective action possible:

> *A counsellor will 'hold' the people until the pain has subsided enough for them to unpack things. We're there to help their confidence and their self-esteem.*
>
> RELATE COUNSELLOR

This is a time when uncertainty about the future means that support is needed by a person who understands without being personally or directly involved. The partners will need objective help in making the decisions, and in carrying them through. Nicky Hart, writing on the passage from marriage to divorce[1], says:

> When important changes of status are negotiated, the participation of experienced people who are sympathetic to the needs of the individual in transit greatly facilitates his movement through the passage. The status passage from being married to being divorced, for a number of reasons, tends to be a very lonely business.

Counselling sporadically gets a bad press, and in 1997 the NHS Centre for Reviews and Dissemination at the University of York concluded that 'counselling, by itself, has not been shown to produce sustained benefit in a variety of groups at risk'. However, counselling must be seen as a partnership between counsellor and client, in which both work together to identify problems and emotions, find and explore options, and facilitate change. It is a useful tool which *enables* an individual or a couple who are *disabled* by pain, conflict or other factors.

The 'cry-for-help' divorce

Sometimes a petition for divorce is in fact an attempt to salvage a marriage; it is a way when all else fails of saying 'Look what's happening to us,' or—frequently—'Please pay attention to me,' or 'What other way forward is there for us?'

Christine
Christine and Martin were a couple in their fifties with three grown-up children. For years Christine had felt no emotional support from Martin, and threatened divorce in an attempt to get him to change. The divorce went through almost against

her wishes, and she sought to get him back. They came to counselling, but Martin had already bought a new house a long way from Christine, and it was this practical factor which in the end made reconciliation impossible.

Divorce, therefore, can be the result of a misguided warning, or a desperate plea—a last-ditch attempt for marital satisfaction, which will usually fail, for it is manipulative and coercive. Only security, trust and communication at a profound level can induce change. A gun at the head, whether it be threats of leaving the conjugal home, or of suicide, are blackmail, and solve none of the underlying problems.

Where are we heading?

For those who are unsure about whether their marriage can be saved, the following questions may help focus the mind and heart:

- What are my needs from this relationship?

- Is there any chance of their being fulfilled?

- What are my spouse's needs?

- Am I or shall I be in any way willing or able to meet them?

- Is my urge to preserve my marriage the result of my fear of being alone?

- Is my urge to end my marriage confused with a desire to 'spread my wings' and 'find myself'?

- When I say, 'I love you' to my partner, do I really mean, 'I need you?'

- Am I prepared to throw away the years of personal, emotional (and material) investment in the marriage?

- If (realistically) things could change with, for example, counselling, will my partner agree to try this?

- Am I willing to try this?

- Do my spouse's good points outweigh the bad?

- If staying together meant moving to a different area, am I flexible enough to do this for the sake of the relationship?

- Are there overriding reasons why a divorce would cause *unbearable* hardship to my partner, or my children, or me?

- Are there overriding reasons why continuing the marriage would cause *unbearable* hardship to my partner, or my children, or me?

- Are there overriding reasons why continuing the marriage would cause *unbearable* hardship to a third party (for example, my child or children with another person)?

- Am I willing to give up any other emotional/sexual attachment?

- Who shall I/my partner/my children become if we divorce?

And finally:

- *Is the pain of being together greater than the pain of being apart?*

Attitudes to saving a marriage have changed. Where once it was thought, by the counselling organizations as well, that it was better for a warring couple, and for their children, to part, now thinking has shifted to 'A bad marriage is better than an ended marriage,' and that the adverse effect of divorce on children is greater than that caused by a parental death.

Only the two people involved can decide whether the marriage should and can be saved. If they decide to try it will be an uphill task with which they will need help and support.

With love, commitment and openness, genuineness, truth, respect, honesty, and the skills of communication and listening, it can be done:

If you really are caring, responsible people it can be sorted out.
DIVORCEE

1. Nicky Hart, *When Marriage Ends: A Study in Status Passage*, Tavistock Publications, 1976.

3

Separation

After he came back he treated me like shit. I was not allowed to talk to him about anything he'd done. In the end I told him to go, and he left—again—in front of the children. After two years he persuaded me to see him, and I lived with him on and off in his flat. He asked me for a lot of money. Then he went back to Tricia. I was beside myself.

Marital breakdown can often be a long, drawn-out process, during which one or both partners can fluctuate between hopes of reconciliation, a continuation of life together, a fresh start, depression, anger, or a desire to be finished with the whole business. Unless one partner insists immediately on finishing the marriage, and divorce is inevitable, a separation can be a limbo time of alternating hope and despair, of resistance or retrenchment or a gradual loosening of the ties that once bound, of looking both backwards and forwards.

The actual decision to divorce may be preceded by one or several separations, when one spouse leaves the family home— either to avoid the other, or to be with a new partner.

It is a time of testing, a period when we will get a glimpse of either the long-term misery, or the relief, which may ultimately be gained by divorce, a time when loneliness may bite for the first time. Without a separation it is possible seriously to underestimate the unhappiness and the practical difficulties that will arise from being apart, and if divorce is sought without this preparation time one or both partners may, one day, long to turn the clock back.

Carol—a disastrous move

Carol was forty when she walked away, in desperation, from her marriage for the first time, though she had had two unhappy affairs before. She started a sexual relationship with a solicitor in the office where she was a part-time secretary and Carol put pressure on the man, Michael, to leave his wife. He acquiesced and rented a house for them in a nearby county town. Carol planned her move, and left home one day while her husband was at work. After one disastrous night in the accommodation, her lover left her and went back to his wife, who was also his partner in the law firm. Carol was devastated, left high and dry in a town where she had no friends, and no longer any job. She longed once again for the comfort and safety of her home, even though she considered her marriage disappointing. For four months her pride prevented her going back, but eventually money ran out, and she did. Her husband—considering he had the moral high ground—refused to discuss their difficulties, or to go to counselling, and Carol continued miserably in a dead marriage.

Freud's writings postulate the theory that the progress of our whole life is toward separation and individuation—first from our mother, and then from our family and home of origin. If these early separations are not fully or satisfactorily achieved during childhood, the separations of adult life will bring back the fear of being abandoned, cut off from security, nurture and safety. If we have not learned to be autonomous adults, we may find ourselves running back to situations that demean or destroy us, solely because we are not capable of being alone.

Dependency of this sort, irrational as it is, explains why some people cannot manage to leave relationships which do them no good at all. Walking away may be a significant first adult step, but it will be a wrench more than many can sustain if they are not ready. For this and other reasons, those who separate from their spouses must be sure of a good support network of friends, relatives, perhaps church or a good counsellor, or—in some cases—refuge or social worker.

Denise—unable to be alone

Denise was a pretty, kind and affectionate girl, but she could not believe anyone could be interested in her. This low self-esteem led her to marry, at 18, her first boyfriend, Vincent. After a while he started drinking heavily and used to beat her up. It took her eight years till she could leave him, and they divorced.

Less than two years later she met and married Clive, who seemed the complete antithesis of Vincent—romantic, dreamy, impulsive. But Clive was unfaithful, was a high spender of money they didn't have, and his sexual gratification depended on Denise performing acts which she found humiliating and deviant. Her opinion of herself was already low, and her body image poor, and she began years of bulimic bingeing and purging. Clive eventually left her for another woman. He divorced Denise, who made a serious suicide attempt.

Once out of hospital, she embarked on two relationships via a dating agency, both of which involved her in deviant sexual acts or suffering drunkenness or violence. She married a third time, a man who was unfaithful. When the affair was discovered Denise begged him on her knees not to leave her.

The dependency of someone like Denise means that even if separation from a bad relationship is achieved by one means or another, there will inevitably be a return to it—or to one like it—until something or someone boosts their self-esteem and confidence sufficiently to attain some autonomy and self-reliance. But all too often those whose self-esteem is minimal are locked in a vicious downward spiral of ever-increasing self-loathing. The research interviews for this book revealed that low self-opinion was typical of women whose husbands both mistreated and left them.

If we have tried every other option, then separation may

bring relief from a situation which is emotionally or sometimes physically painful. Inevitably it will not itself be without pain, but if we are capable of it and if it is carefully thought out, it is a chance to know our heart and mind before the lawyers get to work with an adversarial system which works towards finality:

I was ordered out of the home after two to three weeks. I felt murderous towards her solicitor.

Thelma Fisher, director of National Family Mediation, has said:

It's easy to divorce and once proceedings start, communication between the couple usually ceases. It takes courage… but it is possible to reconstruct… and accept, if not forgive, what might have happened in the past.[1]

The emphasis must be on a separation which is both accepted and worked at by both partners, otherwise it will serve only to exacerbate problems and intensify hurts. The clauses in the Family Law Act 1996 which allow for a 'cooling-off' period before divorce is allowed have the same aim.

James and Michelle—a yo-yo year

James and Michelle, whom we met in the previous chapter, demonstrate that it is no easy thing to dissolve the bond overnight, however thin it has worn. During the course of 12 months, James swung to and fro between his wife and Marie no fewer than nine times, until Marie finally broke under the strain and ended their affair. During this time, too, Michelle was hospitalized twice, emotionally exhausted and indulging in long, alcoholic binges. James attempted a trial separation from Michelle to sort out his feelings, intending not to see Marie either. This did not last, and he again tried some six months later. For months he was a prey to conflicting emotions of longing to be finished with his marriage, extremes of guilt at having left his wife of 24 years, and remorse at what he was inflicting on both his family and his lover. When divorce was decided on, it was not a clean break, with Michelle contesting and blocking everything she could, and—in bitterness—insisting on a settlement that financially crippled James.

Separation is not the same as divorce, and does not inevitably precede it, nor is it an irrevocable move which must signal an ultimate legal termination to the marriage. It will usually involve one partner leaving the matrimonial home—though not necessarily so. One couple, who owned a large and rambling Victorian rectory, managed to lead almost entirely separate lives within the same house, neither eating, sleeping, going out nor talking together. In most houses it would be difficult to do this. Separation has been used as a legal proof that the marriage had broken down irretrievably. In the 1969 divorce legislation two years apart were required for a 'no fault' divorce if both partners consented, or five if one partner refused to accept that the marriage had ended. If one partner walks out then this effectively means that a separation has taken place, but it is not irreversible—legally or in any other way; reconciliation and a return to the home are always possibilities during this period.

Where anger and conflict have escalated to such a level that it is impossible for the couple to be objective, or when couples have grown so distant and disengaged that they cannot 'reconnect' emotionally without help, when one has had an affair, or where one keeps threatening to leave, a trial separation may give a vital breather to everyone in the household from the maelstrom of emotion—or the refrigerator of indifference.

If husband and wife are able to communicate with sufficient kindness and honesty, and can structure the period of separation, with or without the help of a counsellor, it can be a positive time. But to move apart without any direction or guidelines, in anger or despair, achieves little. These separations are usually brief, because guilt, loneliness and fear will bring the two back together, but with nothing resolved (as with James and Michelle, above). 'I promise I'll change' rarely changes anything, and old, dysfunctional patterns will repeat.

Structured trial separations

One counsellor used this metaphor:

You have to tidy up the room before you can go out of the door, and then you go out either separately or together

A structured separation will allow both husband and wife (especially if one partner does not want the marriage to end) some freedom of choice, and an ability to exercise some control over what is happening in their lives. All too often the 'left' spouse feels that events are not of their making, and that a relationship which they believe they have been constructing for years is disintegrating while they stand helplessly watching. Such an agreed separation, in that it is neither a rejection nor a flight, can boost the self-esteem, in that we can come to realize that we can cope, can be independent and self-reliant—perhaps for the first time in our lives.

Each partner can stand back and take a more realistic look at themselves and the relationship, and gauge whether they miss the other sufficiently to return to the relationship out of a sense of belonging rather than fear, guilt or duty. There may be fear, almost panic, about whether the relationship will ever be viable again, and they should, if possible, discuss that with each other, and preferably also with a counsellor or objective third party. But it may also be that with new-found confidence one partner may decide not to return, and the risk is that it may precipitate divorce rather than reconciliation.

A separation such as this would do much to prevent couples divorcing only to find they regret it. This can result in trauma and agony for the man and woman, their children and families. Couples sometimes remarry each other:

> So I divorced him. After that I would see him every weekend when he came back to see Michael. I was doing my degree and started to enjoy being independent. I think he started to respect me more than when I was just a housewife bringing up a child. Divorcing was the best thing that could have happened because it made him realize what he wanted.
>
> *DAILY TELEGRAPH*, 17 NOVEMBER 1994

A separation might provide all these benefits without the trauma of divorce and the costly intervention of solicitors.

Marguerite and Jerry—divorced in haste…

One couple, Marguerite and Jerry, married when they were about thirty, having been part of the same group of friends for many years. The decision to marry was taken quickly, and within three years they had two children. When the children were aged four and three, Marguerite went back to work, angering Jerry who felt her place was at home as a wife and mother. Marguerite then announced she was going to train as a nurse, which was the final straw for her husband. There was a huge row and she told Jerry to go. He started divorce proceedings immediately and within a few months the divorce came through and the house was sold. Then Marguerite seemed to wake up, realize what had happened, and was left with enormous guilt and regret. Jerry himself became bitter and a woman-hater. Ten years on, neither has had another relationship.

In the case of Marguerite and Jerry a carefully-considered separation of a few months might have helped them both decide what they really wanted and what was right for them and their children. It emerged only much later that Marguerite had suffered from post-natal depression for some years after their second daughter was born. A separation could have prevented such an irrevocable decision made on a false basis.

One counsellor said that women will sometimes tell their husbands they want a separation, and say, 'I need my own space for a bit; it's only a trial,' in order to soften the blow of their leaving for good. They fear the man will not be able to cope with the news of the end of the marriage, and so suggest there is still hope.

Ideally, a separation is a time of learning to be single (some people have never actually lived alone), of sorting out finances, negotiating for the children's well-being, of using time creatively, of seeking counselling or therapy to discover why things go wrong and what patterns of behaviour in our lives have not been productive, and of taking responsibility for them, rather than blaming our spouse—or circumstance.

Enforced or unwilling separation

But this is not an ideal world, and in reality this time can be one of the worst that human beings ever have to face:

When she did finally pack her belongings and go, I can only describe it as the worst I've ever felt in my entire life… I didn't know how to live my life any more. Yes, I could cook for myself and all that, but the whole pattern of my life had been shattered—against my will and out of the blue.

When I questioned him about this woman, he just packed his bags and walked out of my life. That's the only way I can describe it. How dare he treat me like that? It shows no respect.

The children had been conceived in love and I still loved their father enough to try and get him back again, even during the year that it took to get the divorce when we were separated and he visited them in our new home.

When a separation is sprung on one partner by the other walking out, often because of a new relationship, they will be knocked for six and will be dealing with hurt, anger, betrayal, shame and pain as well as a thousand practical issues:

> For those who had this decision abruptly foisted upon them, separation constituted a major crisis. They suddenly saw their whole pattern of life crumble around them and a reaction of confusion and despair could scarcely be confined within their domestic selves. Emotional breakdown was common... and many found themselves unable to perform adequately in roles both inside and outside the home[2].

Managing to get up in the morning, see to the children and get to work may be as much as, or more than, many can manage. Blame, recrimination, self-reproach, and 'Why?' will preclude any positive emotions, let alone actions. The first step along the road that leads from 'we' to 'I' can be brutally traumatic.

Loneliness

This time of separation from our spouse, and often from our children and home, whether agreed or not, may be the first time we have lived on our own, away from all that has up till now meant security. Loneliness may bite deep, aggravated by the fact it often occurs in rented accommodation. Even with friends or family we are not part of the everyday bustle of their lives; the chores which once seemed dreary would at least give order and purpose to spare time, and public holidays and weekends drag past, seemingly full of *other* people living in bliss with their spouses and children. Sometimes looking after small children can add to the isolation if finance for a reliable babysitter is a problem, and school hours binding. Pubs, restaurants, cinemas and parks become arenas of solitariness and pain for some separated people.

The ability to be content with our own company is not something everyone possesses. The happiest relationships are made of two people who know how to be alone but choose to be together. This is a time to learn to live apart, to learn the skills which make one independent in practical matters (cooking, changing electrical plugs or car wheels, putting up shelves, ironing, sewing), but none of this is easy when our emotions have been whipped raw, and depression or exhaustion mean it is hard to do the bare minimum.

It is undeniable that with a divorce rate nudging 40 per cent, a large proportion of the people we meet will either be about to divorce, in the process of doing so or will be emerging from it. That means there are many others also experiencing the pangs and practicalities of loneliness at the same moment as we ourselves are. There are, of course, many clubs and societies for those separated or divorced, but the dictum 'Needy people need needy people' should not be forgotten, and a quick fix of 'togetherness' with someone else in the same boat will not necessarily bring happiness in the long run until our marriage has been properly mourned, and the issues that destroyed it explored and resolved.

Separation after violence

It's so nice not to have to face the continual criticism and the continual violence. Once it was so bad... I felt that was the bottom line. He left and I didn't try to get him back. After two years I said we have been separated for two years but he wouldn't divorce. After five years it could have been done within the space of one month and have cost very little, but he wouldn't agree. I kept telling people he was away on business.

When there is physical, sexual or emotional violence there may be no option but to leave, and this can sometimes happen without having had time to make plans. Our own safety and that of the children are paramount. But so often added to all the other difficulties encountered by those separating from their spouse are those of protection, lodging, finance, legal proceedings, constant flight and fear. For those who are being accused of violence there can be additional burdens of guilt, shame, remorse and fear to labour under.

Separation after adultery

About a week after she left me she phoned and we had a conversation and she was quite lighthearted, telling me she had been out for a drink with her boyfriend's friends, and I found it so painful. I was distraught.

After 20 years of marriage there was a separation—four years before the final split. I was very shocked. He'd been involved with somebody for a number of years. There was a big confrontation. I went to a solicitor and started a divorce—I thought if he saw I was serious he might stop. But he asked to come back. Two years later I kicked him out again as it had started up again.

Shattered trust means not only betrayal of promises, it spreads its poison over memories of good times as well. It is a bitter pill to swallow, when our spouse leaves because of a relationship with someone else.

It can be a bewildering and painful experience for the adulterous spouse as well. Events may have moved fast and beyond their control once the affair or relationship is discovered or confessed. They may find themselves told to go—or abandoned. The adulterous relationship may not be what they want; it may have been the result of many pressures and of a deteriorating marriage, but there will often be intense guilt and remorse, and the disapproval of family and friends. It can be intensely lonely.

The family and marital therapist Liberty Kovacs[3] recommends group therapy as helpful in these circumstances, for there will be feedback from others who have experienced similar trauma. It helps to know we are not as different as we may think, and that someone who has an affair is not necessarily a monster who sets out to destroy the family. Nevertheless, this is a painful time, for guilt corrodes and affects all our interpersonal dealings, and we may have to come to terms with the fact that our behaviour has killed the marriage.

Some never move beyond separation. They live their lives apart, entirely independent of each other, without taking the final step to divorce. If there is no third party involved, or if there are religious scruples, then there may be no final legal resolution. Nicky Hart[4] writes:

> Whereas elaborate customs exist to help widows in their time of grief or to programme brides through the passage into a married state, the newly separated person must usually sort out his problems alone… The participant in a status passage from married to formerly married may be locked in the *période de marge* for an indefinite time. This prolonged state of marginality in between statuses, unsure of the outcome, and in a sense 'outside society'—is highly conducive of [sic] personal distress and may contribute directly to the trauma associated with separation and divorce.

Such an ending, unformalized, will be more likely to leave unfinished emotional business between the former partners. Unfinished business militates against the healing of the wounds which the death—slow or sudden—of the relationship can cause.

1. From an interview with the author, October 1996.

2. From the paper by Nicky Hart, 'Contrasts and correspondences in the meaning of marital breakdown for men and women', given to the 1974 Conference of the British Sociological Society on Sexual Divisions and Society.

3. Liberty Kovacs *Separateness/Togetherness: A paradox in relationships*, Journal of Couples Therapy (The Haworth Press Inc) vol 4, 1994, no 3/4, pp 83–94.

4. Nicky Hart *When Marriage Ends: A Study in Status Passage*, Tavistock Publications, 1976.

4

The decision to divorce

They were divorced as quickly as they had married. She said she just woke up one morning and she was divorced. Then she realized what a terrible thing had happened. She desperately wanted to go back, but he was not to be moved. He said if it weren't for the children he'd be happy never to set eyes on her again.

MARRIAGE COUNSELLOR

We were separated for six years before we divorced—then when he wanted a reason to divorce me the grounds were 'unreasonable behaviour'—that's because I had been homesick in South Africa!

If reconciliation is not possible, and we are not willing to live our lives together, then at some stage a point will be reached where a decision is made to divorce. Usually there is one partner who desires divorce more than the other, but that in itself can sometimes so ruin the relationship for the other that they, too, in the end may accept the termination of the marriage:

I did manage to let the better, more forgiving feelings come to the fore, and—after 18 months of trying to hold the marriage together—decided that the best thing would be to get a divorce with the least recrimination possible and allow my husband to seek happiness with the woman he loved.

I said to him, 'If you want your divorce you can have it. If you want to be with her, go. We don't want a lot of acrimony.'

But it is usually, and self-evidently, the partner who does not wish to lose the marriage who has difficulty accepting that the moment has come. However, both partners (unless there is a ready-made relationship to go to) may shy away from this new and threatening situation which places them at risk of major change. Splitting up may seem attractive, but it must—if the people involved are honest—bring with it a review and reappraisal of their identity and system of relating at an intimate level. Such a process is painful and there is a personal price to pay, so in the end the couple may decide: 'better the devil we know…'

That is why separation, if it is is not necessarily the precursor to divorce and is used to explore what is involved, can serve as a good preparation for the final outcome. The better prepared we are for the end and for its implications in personal and practical terms, the readier we shall be to accept it, however hard it is.

What holds people back?

Other, more practical, reasons may cause one partner to fight the end of the marriage, refusing to accept the inevitable and heart-breaking changes:

Sam and Emma

Sam (32) and Emma (33) had been married four years and had two children aged six months and two years. The couple were both graduates, and had well-paid professional jobs. They had lived together for three years before marrying, but now felt their relationship was dead and that there was little in common to bind them other than parenting. Sam however, vigorously opposed divorce. He feared strongly (and with some statistical evidence to back him up, since men who lose custody of their children frequently lose touch with them altogether in the years following divorce) that he would lose his children, and this would have been for him an unbearable blow.

The whole question of the children of the marriage is, of course, enormously influential in the decision whether to divorce, and has also considerable bearing on the feelings their parents will be prey to afterwards.

For the husband or wife who arrives home one day to a *fait accompli*—a note on the mantelpiece, or an empty house—there may have been no time of adjustment whatsoever. We may think, or even hope, we know that our spouse will regret what they have done, that their new relationship will not last, that they will come back and beg; but truth must be faced one day. Relationships—like people—die. There may come a moment when the life support machine must be turned off, the tubes disconnected, and what once was is no more.

If there is no other way…

If one or other partner—or both—are determined that there is no chance that the marriage can be brought to life again, then divorce is usually the answer. As in most things pertaining to human relationships, what is now important is *how* we go about it. The process of disengagement is as important as the outcome for both parties, for their children, and for any future relationship they may make.[1]

'I hate you, but you're the children's father'

Fiona and Duncan were at daggers drawn. In the process of deciding to end their conflictual marriage she had not a good word to say about him, and was so full of resentment and anger that divorce was inevitable. Yet Fiona was determined never to say anything bad to her two young children about their father, so that they should go on loving him. In spite of her excruciating feelings of bitterness she was able to say to Duncan 'You'll always be my children's father; come round any time.'

If, like Fiona, couples in the turmoil of deciding to split can separate their feelings from the situation then they ease their own way forward and give their children more positive messages which limit the scarring of parental breakup.

It is rare that a decision to part is clear-cut. We have seen some of the reasons (psychological, practical) why, for some people, however unfulfilling the union, the decision to terminate it may not be made.

The decision to divorce—men and women

He insisted that he wanted the marriage to continue and that he didn't want a life with his mistress. He insisted that. But it was the lies I couldn't stand, not the infidelity.

In very broad terms men are more happy for the marriage to carry on as it has always done, and it is statistically true that more women petition for divorce than men. Marriage suits men, and we explore the differing effects of divorce on men and women in Chapter 9. Men have lower expectations of emotional satisfaction, and rather desire a pleasant shared life. Thus, a recognition that emotional needs are going unsatisfied tends to be more on the wife's side. Once a woman is certain that she will never get what she wants within it, there is a strong chance she will veer away from the marriage relationship, and divorce may follow. This is a fairly common phenomenon of divorces which occur after five or ten years of marriage (one of the statistically highest-risk times) when couples have married young. *He* imagines everything is going along fine, but *she* grows up more than he, becomes mature, cultured, aware, emotionally literate, and knows there is something wrong.

Paradoxically, the shock of divorce can change this unwillingness to be in touch with our emotions, if we let it:

Sonia and Adrian

Sonia and Adrian married in their mid-twenties and parted before they were thirty, still childless. It was Sonia's idea to have a trial separation, for she was disappointed with her husband and her marriage. They had married without exploring their expectations of each other, and now she felt that Adrian had failed to be the husband she thought he was going to be. He, absorbed in building his career, had refused to hear her complaints. She left suddenly and was equally suddenly lost without the secure base of marriage, knowing she hadn't wanted to stay but not being able to define what she had lost. Adrian was jolted into working on himself by the suddenness of Sonia's going. He found a personal counsellor, and started to look at what had been happening over the previous few years.

The 'empty nest' and divorce

Women may also be gripped by agonizing uncertainty about whether to end a marriage, surprisingly, when it has endured half a lifetime. This is 'empty nest' time, when the children have grown up and gone, and a less than completely fulfilled woman has more time for herself, and hopes to 'find herself' for the first time in her existence. Then separation may not give a complete enough psychological break, and she may feel driven to divorce.

The mid-life crisis and divorce

This, too, is the age when men, in the grips of what is called the 'mid-life crisis'—'le démon de midi', seek the rejuvenating effects of new love and sexual pleasure with a younger woman. Men who decide to leave their wives for this reason may undergo considerable suffering and tension as they swing to and fro between guilt, remorse and the lure of someone who makes them feel young and potent:

I thought, 'Here we have a man in the middle of a mid-life crisis. He's lost his job, he's going to lose his house.' He took on a completely new personality. It was classic—just before he was fifty. It was like another, different person. It was horrendous. He accused me of trying to poison his food. It's like he closed the door on this part of his life. It was the only way he could cope with what he'd done—to make me invisible.

He said 'I'm going to start a new life with her. Nothing in my old life will ever affect me again.'

Once they have left uncertainty behind and chosen to leave their partner of twenty or thirty years, they may unconsciously deny the havoc they have wreaked, but they may also have to bear the opposition of their children, and not a little opprobrium:

My daughter said: 'I have to accept I'll never get my father back. He'll never be the same man I knew. He won't ever change.'

The uncertainty in one partner and their unilateral wish to get out of the marriage bond will inevitably trigger tremendous soul-searching and deliberation, carried on with or without the knowledge of the spouse. It can happen that these processes of reflection result in a decision not to terminate the relationship, since a consideration of the strengths of the existing marriage and an assessment of what will be lost if divorce ensues may be sufficient for the one who is dissatisfied to draw back from the brink:

■ possible loneliness;

■ recurring pain;

■ the agony of the children and their possible loss to one parent;

■ financial difficulties;

- the constant knowledge of failure;

- the potential departure of friends and maybe family who either try to remain impartial, or who side with the other;

- the breaking of vows.

All these must be weighed against the current difficulties and pain in the relationship itself. It is not a light decision.

If uncertainty prevails then the one who wishes to leave may consciously withdraw their emotional investment from the relationship, perhaps hoping it will wither and fade away. It may, if their spouse then matches the emotional withdrawal with a corresponding decrease in involvement. But if they respond by stepping up their commitment to and investment in the marriage, it will result in a painful stalemate. Another result is that the second partner may also feel so hurt and angry about the behaviour of the first one who wishes to leave, that they move to terminate the relationship, causing distress to the first partner.

It is inevitable that a sustained wish to terminate a relationship, on one or both sides—whatever the formal outcome—must spoil that relationship, since it shatters the illusion of their solidarity. There seems little hope that this period of indecision, of doubt, of searing and tearing apart and perhaps trying 'one more time' and then 'once more', can be anything but agony.

Ultimately the uncertainty will end, and the decision to end the marriage will be taken because—for one partner at least—the pain of living together is so great that it is less painful to be apart. The emotional disengagement which may have started years before will now formalize itself into physical disengagement. The couple will decide to separate, and apply for a formal end to the marriage.

What is certain is that the decision to stop being a couple is almost never painless, and that the loss of our previous life and partner will not just happen without paying the price of a jumble of conflicting emotions: confusion, doubt, pain, guilt, remorse, anger, fear, loneliness and—ultimately—resignation and acceptance. There will be wounds which leave scars. And the practical consequences of the decision will themselves, in turn, bring emotional pain and turmoil. It is these consequences and emotions, and the process of going through them, that we explore in Part 2.

1. Appendix 1 deals with the 1996 Family Law Act, which introduces new divorce legislation, and which will come into force in 1999. It also looks at the process of mediation, recommended in the new Act, and how this can help the process of divorce.

PART 2

The wounds of divorce

Introduction

How much water
would it take
to wash away these hurts?
Is the well inside me
deep enough
to cleanse them?

Or would a meagre trickle
simply soften the surface of the wound
to greater helplessness?
How do we estimate
our own defences?

FROM A POEM BY TANYA PALMER 'WOULD CRYING HELP?'

Divorce is not one finite event; it is a gradual and usually intensely painful process of dissolving psychological, emotional and social bonds, and of mourning these, the roles that went with them, and (perhaps) the person we shared them with.

The severity of the pain we experience will depend on what we lose, and to a large degree whether we initiated or desired the divorce. The factors contributing to our distress include: the degree of attachment we feel for our partner, the closeness we have experienced with them, our own autonomy as adult human beings, the length of time the marriage has existed, custody of any children, and issues of finance, domicile, and support networks.

The process of divorcing brings us face to face with the reality of ourselves as never before, and what we see in the mirror can be a shock for which life so far has not prepared us. It is therefore not only a time of losing a relationship, a spouse, sometimes our children, our home and friends, but also a time when we have to adapt to the loss of our own and often cherished self-image.

It is a bridging time when we must say goodbye to much that was precious, depended upon, clung to, and during which we are forced to cross—often with great difficulty—to a different place, with a different map, different terrain and different inhabitants.

This second section of the book helps provide a route map for the transition which the divorcing person makes from one state to another, from partnership to singleness. It reflects the second, middle, stage of any rite of passage—that between separation and incorporation.

Because there is usually one partner who wishes to terminate the marriage more than the other (though this may not be the one who petitions for divorce), we shall look at this process both from the point of view of the one who leaves the marriage and the one left—the 'loser'. We shall also look at the significant differences in the way men and women react to and deal with the divorce process and the emotions it engenders.

In this section we also explore the social dimension of divorce, for just as marriage is a commitment to permanent relationship in the eyes of society, so its dissolution will in turn exercise some effect on society. Society too will affect those who are divorcing or have divorced: family and friends may fall away or their loyalties be divided; there may be social stigma, all at a time when support from outside the relationship is vital to coping. Finally we mention the influence of the major religious faiths on the life of a divorcee.

Divorce may be a passage from relative security to insecurity, from an established lifestyle to emotional and material chaos— or it may spell tranquillity and relief; but inevitably it will be a time of questioning and taking stock, of experimenting with new behaviours, of changing patterns and maybe of changing values and outlook. It is an enforced movement from one set of circumstances to another; it terminates the existing life structure and creates the necessity for another.

The major part of this middle section provides a sort of guide through the process of transition, a map of the emotional landscape of divorce which draws on the experience and feelings of those who have travelled this way. We look at the stages of transition and loss—from the shock of breakdown and the decision to divorce through to a tolerable degree of acceptance and the resumption of control over our life and emotions, though it must be acknowledged that many will remain imprisoned in their 'life sentence' of rejection and low self-esteem.

5

A life sentence? The consequences of divorce

It's a total life sentence. This will go on till I die... I have to deal with the past and the present and the future. It's a total life sentence.

The 'life sentence', as divorce is perceived by many divorcees, not only has a bearing on our lives in terms of its duration, but is something which invades every aspect of daily living. While the emotional effects of marital breakup are raging within us, the practical consequences of the divorce will in turn be affecting us, our lives and feelings. Often in a vicious downward spiral, practical issues will modify moods, and our psychological state affects how we deal with the practicalities. Even for those who wish to be free of their marriage, the consequences of liberation are inescapable. In this chapter[1] we examine the major areas in which divorce marks our whole existence, before turning (in Chapter 6) to a detailed examination of the emotions themselves.

How long?

The pain occasioned by divorce can be so intense that those on the receiving end will cry out, 'How long must I suffer?' Healing can seem slow, non-existent sometimes.

The consequences of divorce can indeed be life long. One research sample[2] of a group of divorced men suggested that the 'disastrous' effects of divorce can be permanent, and that their longevity can be as destructive as their severity. It seemed in that particular sample that those who thought the effects had been extremely damaging were those who were also the slowest to recover. Another study[3] of divorced women, ten years after the split, says:

> The interviews were painful to many. While clearly not as painful as on earlier occasions, the ten years had not fully erased significant residues of the failed marital relationship or vivid memories of the pre-existing family and of the divorce.

Intensity

Suffering occurs whenever attachment is present.[4]

The type and intensity of the pain brought about by dissolving the bond of marriage will depend on the marriage itself, and how long it has existed. The ties that bind, and which are so painful and so messy to cut, are formed by shared and ongoing experiences and projects, habit and routine forged together over the years which create an interdependency, intimate knowledge, private language, and even predictability. These bonds (the 'glue' of the marriage) grow, and remain—however thin—during times of tension and conflict. All this is dismantled by divorce, and the longer the marriage has lasted, the greater the number of these ties which have to be severed:

> ... he felt like sitting down with her and sharing a bottle of wine. Letting her make him a fried egg sandwich and having a giggle over some of those tapes of American sitcoms they had enjoyed together. He remembered how her glasses would suddenly glint with excitement, when

he suggested an unscheduled bottle of wine, and how relaxed she looked when they were having a quiet evening in…

TANYA PALMER, FROM A SHORT STORY, 'SUBJECTIVE VIEW'

Statistically, marriages which break up in the first few years account for approximately 30—40 per cent of all divorces. Once the bond has been strongly cemented by years of conjugality then marital breakdown will provoke tremendous feelings of failure and possibly rejection, which can be overwhelming, and grief that is long-lived and intense on both sides. Where our emotional investment in a terminated relationship was a heavy one, this is unavoidable. The pain is perhaps greatest where one partner is still emotionally engaged and in love with the other, who may be indifferent, cold, angry or already in a new relationship. For those who have over many years established habits and roles, a longstanding social network, and a whole gamut of shared experience and emotion, the destruction of these is devastating.

Deprivation

Marriage can bring us many positive benefits. Among them will be a sense of identity and worth, help and support, the opportunity for nurture and growth, and emotional and social integration. It may also bring economic security. Those who divorce and become single, without a new partner to go to, will lose all this, and will also suffer from the breakup of their personal, social network where the connection to it came primarily through their partner. The routine of daily life changes and this disorients us, cutting us off from familiar structures, surroundings and habits. In short we are deprived of almost everything that made our life what it was and brought us order, comfort and pleasure.

Sexual deprivation

What I miss most about marriage is being cuddled.

Divorce may bring us (if the terminal stages of marriage have not already) a sexual bereavement. For some, in shock and grief, sex may be the last thing they seek at this time; for others its cessation means the loss of comfort and a sense of value. Some will search for these benefits in transient sexual encounters which, of their very nature, produce the opposite effect.

Grief

Grief includes a sense of rejection, hurt, sadness, self-pity, shame, guilt, anger, doubt and low self-esteem which are commonly experienced by both partners in varying degrees. We grieve for all we have lost, though initially it is almost impossible to analyse the accumulation of pain, and know what we are mourning.

Injustice

A burning sense of injustice can fuel the fires of hurt and grief, sometimes promoting a desire for vengeance and getting even with the person who has betrayed the vows, the relationship and us.

I was made destitute by my divorce, plus a legal battle against lawyers and a biased judge over the next nine years... Am I bitter? Yes, because I did not get justice.

One of the most heartbreaking things was watching that man with whom I'd had children stand up in court and try and get away with it, and giving me so very little in my middle and old age.

He had my parents' money and the villa. He took me to court. He destroyed me. He spent £100,000 with her—they went everywhere, did everything

Anti-social behaviour

When we are full of pain we will often find inappropriate ways of getting rid of it. We project it on to others, especially our 'ex', hating them rather than the pain, or what is within us. In the throes of anger and jealousy we can go berserk, drinking heavily or being violent, inflicting damage on whatever or whoever crosses our path. In recent years the newspapers have featured accounts of jealous husbands and wives—wrecking expensive cars, cutting off a penis, stalking with a machete. Violent assault is not uncommon.

Self-esteem

Few people getting married expect to divorce, though statistics suggest that we should not consider ourselves exempt from the possibility. If our marriage does break down, and cannot or will not be repaired, the experience almost invariably entails a sense of personal failure. It is a bruising and a battering time for our sense of self and its value. If our self-image does emerge unscathed, it may be that we are denying the full impact of the breakdown, or trying to shovel the blame for it wholly on to the other person.

When we lose something that was important to us self-confidence can take a knock; self-esteem is ground into nothingness by guilt and remorse, by being blamed or rejected. When our self-esteem is under attack we often seek ways of boosting our image of ourselves, quick fixes which may not be productive or appropriate for the stage of grieving which we have reached:

After Jonathan left me I had to prove at all costs that I was still attractive. I was stupid, reckless, and had a series of encounters—that is the only word—that were not only brief but bitter. I finally realized I'd do better to spend more time with my children and pay them some attention while I was waiting for the right person to appear in my life.

... a permanent, ranting desire to eat, to seek out comforting pies and puddings and buns and cakes. The more she hated herself, the more she desired to shore up her bulk with carbohydrates.

TANYA PALMER, 'SUBJECTIVE VIEW'

Some are able to take a longer view:

Two failures is two too many. If there's ever another time I want it to work. So—instead of rushing in like I did after my first divorce—I'm taking things slowly, and I'm having psychotherapy to find out what these patterns and needs are in my life, and that helps a lot.

Public opinion

Any party to a terminated or even a spoiled relationship is tarred by failure and... regarded as somehow odd, deficient, or deviant.[5]

Before our belief in ourself rises from the ashes of our previous relationship, we may be a prey to persisting and crippling feelings that we have failed society as well—for marriage tends to be seen by the outside world as either 'success' or 'failure'. This perception of stigma, which reduces still further our self-esteem, adds to our grief and intensifies it, for it diminishes our ability to seek support, even from family and friends. We examine the social dimension in Chapter 7.

Standard of living

When husband and wife part, the standard of living of both is likely to decline. The one who has custody of the children (and in the majority of cases this is still the mother) will find their budget strained. Despite the creation of the notorious Child Support Agency and despite court orders, many fathers get away without paying regular maintenance, and those who did not choose to divorce and who are perhaps all but cut off from their children may be tempted to stop maintenance payments. Inevitably one or both will suffer financially.

If maintenance is not forthcoming, a divorced mother must choose between going out to work to support her children—with the strain of juggling timetables, and the cost and worry of finding reliable childminders—and applying for State benefits in order to say at home to look after them:

> I agreed to accept only what I thought reasonable and to return to work with paid childcare… Financially, my life has been a disaster—earning far less now than I did as a 25-year-old. Life over the last twenty years has been very hard and tough—though he never defaulted on the maintenance payments. I totally missed out on the boom years.

Fathers, too, may be forced to give up work and to rely on state handouts if they are left with small children.

If the family home is sold both former partners may find themselves with a sum insufficient for their needs, especially so if one has care of the children or has taken on a relationship with new family obligations. It is rare that one spouse earns sufficient to provide comfortably for two families. Where the custodial parent retains the family home there will be little capital to play with, while sometimes the non-custodial parent can find themselves in the loneliness and emotional sterility of rented accommodation.

Relocation

Divorce, as we have seen above, means that at least one partner will have to set up a new home. Here they may be torn between—on the one hand—the desire to shake the dust of the marriage off their feet, and move to a part of the country where there are no memories, no stigma, and no chance of meeting their ex-spouse with a new lover or family, and—on the other— the ties of work, other family members, or a desperate desire to stay geographically close to their children:

> I do think it's vital the child has regular contact with both parents… there isn't a day goes by that I don't think about Samantha. Leaving her was the hardest thing I have ever, ever done—You never really get used to it. I moved nearby and made sure she could visit me. Eventually I got a house not far from Samantha.
>
> 'NON-CUSTODIAL' MOTHER QUOTED IN THE *DAILY MAIL*, 21 NOVEMBER, 1996

When a geographical move is forced upon us, the uprooting can make for quite severe psychological, if not material, hardship. It is no light thing—after maybe half a lifetime, and (in the case of older divorcees) heavy dependence on their role as spouse and their social identity—to up sticks for a new life somewhere else.

Ellen
Ellen, in her seventies, was left by her husband who was, he said, making 'a last bid for freedom'. Ellen was forced to move from their comfortable bungalow to rented accommodation in a nearby town, thus losing touch with her neighbours and all the support systems she knew.

Many interviewees spoke of the agony of moving after a divorce:

I had to go and I did go. I didn't have anywhere to go. I took what I could carry.

I've been homeless for the past few months. This has made more painful the loss of our family home, which was beautiful.

I was totally bereft; it was the loss of the house, I suppose, and all my roots.

Some, who could wait until they were emotionally ready for the break with the past, saw it as symbolic of a new beginning:

Full of hope she sped down the motorway to London, the little understanding house, the garden, the future. There was simply too much invested in all this to allow it to fail. The secret of survival is in moving, and the more decisive the move, the greater the potential for beginning again. 'This time', she told herself, 'I'll get it right.'

FROM 'MOVING' BY TANYA PALMER

but others were 'untimely ripped' from the womb of their former security, and suffered acutely.

Domestic roles and family life

Suddenly, when we separate from our spouse, we lose our role within the household. We are no longer a wife or husband. We may retain some domestic and family role as mother or father, or we may create a new role in a new household, but often the need for our particular skills and tasks disappears—no one needs us to put up shelves, change the oil filter, or cut wood; no one needs our cooking night after night, or our memory about paying bills. We feel deskilled, roleless, useless. Self-esteem ebbs further away, and yet at the same time we may have to struggle with unfamiliar tasks which—because of general depression—may at that time be beyond us.

When we are newly, and perhaps suddenly, single the routines that have structured our existence are meaningless:

> All the ideas she ever had about what she would do if she had the time, if she did not have to fit her activity around his prowling, edgy existence, have disappeared, or appear simply pointless. Her relationship to everything and everyone has changed. She does not feel entitled to wear her wedding ring but its absence makes her hand strangely light.
>
> FROM 'SUBJECTIVE VIEW' BY TANYA PALMER

This diminishes our sense of usefulness and identity.

Professional life

During the earlier stages of our coming to terms with the loss of our marriage it is not unlikely that our performance at work will be impaired by what is going on both around us and inside us. Absenteeism is high and concentration low when our world is crashing around us:

> *I couldn't think of anything else, and I couldn't sleep. I was completely rocked.*

It may be that we encounter considerably less sympathy at work than those who have been bereaved through death. Indeed, it was felt by some that divorcees were discriminated against in the job market. This may be because of unreliability (coping with crises, coping as a single parent, court appearances), illness (see page 93), or in some cases it was felt that divorce was a sign of psychological instability.

In the early phases of separation and marital termination, emotional breakdown is frequent, and this is almost impossible to contain without its affecting every area of life. Work, if we have it, is bound to suffer.

Women who have worked during their marriage and raised a family at the same time may find that the juggling with which career mothers are all too familiar is possible only when supported by a husband's presence. Women who have not worked for some years because they have been at home looking after children may not find it easy to get back into the job market, let alone get their feet back on any career ladder. So they are forced to take any job they can find, regardless of its compatibility with school hours and holidays.

Nevertheless, there are those who can find in their job a sense of self-worth, as well as a means of economic survival, which is anodyne:

> It wasn't until my marriage broke up that I began to take it [my job] seriously, because it was all I had left. It distracted me from everything else that was going on in my life.
>
> JULIA CARLING, QUOTED IN THE *DAILY TELEGRAPH*, 27 JANUARY, 1997

> *Once I had a job I had to jolly well get on with it, and that was my salvation, really, my job.*

Social identity

The many different and complex aspects of our social, professional and domestic existence which are affected by divorce will combine to produce a cumulative effect on our roles and relationships. The loss of our marriage can disrupt, often for a long time, our social identity and attack our very selves.

Our social identity is made up of a combination of professional, family, marital, domestic and other roles and relationships. If we have invested heavily in our marital role then the gap left by it on divorce will be immense, and our sense of identity may be lost for a time:

My marriage was everything to me, just everything. It was a total, utter commitment. I had no problem about this. I was determined it would work beyond all measure.

Up until the last quarter of the twentieth century (and probably still, for conditioning dies hard) marriage usually made up a large part of a woman's social identity, for the conjugal role has normally been dominant even for those women who work. Certainly for older wives, who have known little but running the home, raising children, and looking after their husbands, the passing of their marital status is devastating. Men who consider themselves as 'breadwinners' for the family, and see that as their primary role, will also find it hard to adjust to the disappearance of their social identity, and those who lose their children will lose doubly: for them life will be meaningless unless some substitute identity can be found.

The less individuals have been free to invest in other interests and relationships outside the marriage, the fewer resources they will have, and the more they will suffer this loss of identity:

Charlotte had an idea of what she wanted her life to be, and would be reluctant to involve herself with my life. She wasn't interested in my things, and so I didn't pursue them.

Loss of social identity is inevitably more acute in the earlier phase of divorcing before readjustment can take place, At this time when our immediate world has fallen in ruins, the past seems sullied and the investment we made in it is now seen as a waste. The future has no direction or purpose. Quite simply all that made for our identity may have disappeared. Now it is 'I' instead of 'we', 'I' am reduced to nothingness. This is particularly true of long-term marriages where one spouse abruptly deserts the partner of twenty or thirty years or so, and readjustment is far less likely in these cases, where the abandoned spouse may never emerge from the yearning or depressed stage of grief. Even those who have voluntarily left the marriage may be surprised at their loss of identity. Tolstoy, as we saw, left his life-long marriage in his early eighties, but died alone a few days later.

In some cases the letting go of a stifling relationship can aid us to find out who we are:

Conrad and Dana

Conrad married Dana, whom he had met at university, and he went on to become a successful businessman. Twenty years on he described his marriage as being 'a walk-on part'. Coming towards mid-life, he realized that all he did was speak the lines his wife dictated, and the only way he could deal with it was to walk out. He felt there was no other way to find, and assert, his individuality. In business he knew who he was, but at home, he said, he had 'an absolute sense of who he wasn't'.

Health[6]

The new legislation on divorce, the Family Law Act, which comes into effect in 1999, can be seen as a sort of Government Health Warning: 'Divorce can seriously damage your health'. There is widespread evidence that one of the primary effects of the breakup of the marriage and family is a deterioration in both psychological and physical wellbeing, and that the local doctor is one of the first in line to witness the results of relational stress.

Stress

Difficult life events figure on a 'stress' scale. But divorcing, as we have seen, is not merely an event, but a process which is ongoing until (if ever) we can readjust. Coping with conflict and perhaps violence, then the loss of our partner, the marriage and our status is traumatic enough, but when we have added to it moving house, financial problems, difficulties with our children or loss of them, problems at work, it adds up to a crushing and constant pressure.

Premature death

This is no exaggeration. There is a strong relationship between marital breakdown and premature death, with divorced men in particular running a substantially higher risk of dying earlier than married men. This may in part result from excessive drinking (three times as many divorced men as married men drink more than fifty units of alcohol per week), increased smoking, and unsafe sex (divorced men tend to have frequent and transitory sexual encounters and are less likely to use condoms than other groups).

Accidents

But that fall, that stupid clumsy fall was the last straw.

Evidence also points to the fact that the divorced and separated are more at risk than their married or single counterparts—a factor to consider in evaluating the death of Diana, Princess of Wales. A One plus One booklet[7], based on current statistics, tells us:

Road traffic accidents, falls and deaths through fire and drowning are all more common in the divorced population... It is possible that some of these accidents are self-inflicted, but in most cases they are not. Why should those who have experienced marital breakdown be more accident-prone? The first answer is alcohol. A large proportion of accidents are alcohol-related, and increased drinking is a very common response to marriage breakdown. Secondly, marital breakdown often leads to an impaired ability to concentrate, and to tiredness and lowered performance. These factors are also associated with increased risk of accidental injury.

Other bad news for divorcees is:

■ They are more likely to die of heart disease (and divorced men twice as likely) than those who are married.

■ Cancer survival rates are markedly poorer.

■ Divorced and separated men are twice as likely to die of non-smoking-related cancers.

■ The rise in suicides has been greater.

Illness

The various stages which we have looked at (shock, anxiety, anger, longing, grief, depression) will often manifest themselves in a variety of physical symptoms. Typical among them are headaches, migraines, muscular tension, insomnia, loss of appetite or 'comfort' eating, cardiac irregularities, indigestion, respiratory difficulties, diarrhoea or constipation, dry skin and extreme fatigue.

Depression

As we shall see in the next chapter, depression is one of the stages of loss, and it is one at which many will stick for months if not years. One study[8] found that men who experienced divorce or separation were 9.3 times and women 3.1 times more likely to experience a major depression than were happily married men and women. Men who divorced were likely to be depressed for the first time. In the research interviews, very few subjects had not known depression of some sort, and/or anxiety, irritability, tension, mood swings, fatigue, insomnia and general malaise or dysfunction. Suicide or suicidal gestures increase when we lose an attachment figure, for with this person disappear all the familiar structures which make up our lives and give them meaning and worth.

It is against this background of the psychological, physical and practical effects of divorce, each one affecting the others, that we struggle to come to terms with what we have lost.

1. Some of the categories identified in this chapter come from the paper by Nicky Hart: 'Contrasts and correspondences in the meaning of marital breakdown for men and women', given to the 1974 Conference of the British Sociological Society on Sexual Divisions and Society.
2. Peter Ambrose, John Harper, Richard Pemberton, *Surviving Divorce, Men beyond Marriage*, Wheatsheaf Books, 1983.
3. Judith Wallerstein, *Women after Divorce: Preliminary report from a Ten-Year Follow-Up*, American Journal of Orthopsychiatry, 56 [1], January 1986.
4. Jack Dominian, *Marriage—making or breaking*, A British Medical Association Publication, 1987.
5. George J. McCall, in *Personal Relationships 4: dissolving personal relationship*, ed. S. Duck, Academic Press, 1982.
6. Data from *Marital Breakdown and the Health of the Nation*, ed. Fiona McAllister, One plus One, 1995 (second edition).
7. *Marital Breakdown and the Health of the Nation* (see above), p. 23
8. Livingston, Bruce and Kim, 1992, 'Differences in the effects of Divorce on Major depression in Men and Women', American Journal of Psychiatry, 149.7.914 (quoted in *Marital Breakdown and the Health of the Nation,* as above.)

6

The emotions of divorce

It is like a bereavement. You have to move on. After a while I thought I have to stand on my own two feet. You can't go on being a poor and pathetic single woman. But I still find it hurtful when I meet people we used to know and they think, 'She's got over it.' But I haven't. I really don't think I have.

When we lose something of significance, even if it is by our own design or fault that we lose it, we grieve for it. If this something is of the magnitude of our marriage, which makes up the fabric of our daily life and into which all else is woven, we must let this mourning take its full course. Even if we are relieved to be out of it, or even if we wish to be with someone else, we have lost or left something which was part of ourselves. And for those whose divorce entails loss of status, role, structure, security, home, children—*and* the person we have loved—the bereavement may be intense.

Grieving, like divorce, is a transitional process, the bridge over which we cross from the breakup of the marriage to a place of acceptance from which we can move on less painfully. In crossing this bridge we gradually and with increasing accuracy process the information—the marriage is dead—and come to terms with what we have lost. The transition is made up of a number of stages, whose purpose evolves as time—and we— progress. At first they protect us from knowledge which may be too painful to contemplate immediately, then they spur us on to recover the person or thing we have lost, and finally they help us face the pain, assimilate it, and move on.

As those who are experienced in bereavement through death

may understand, recovery from the cutting short of a harmonious and loving relationship, in the course of which we subsume the good into ourselves, is usually easier. We may mourn acutely, but there is little of the guilt, ambivalence and negativity which often results from the cessation of an unproductive and unfulfilling relationship. It is axiomatic that divorce does not usually follow a satisfactory and satisfying relationship.

The stages of loss

There are a number of theories on the stages of loss, and these are sketched out in Appendix 2. People, however, are human and idiosyncratic, and do not mourn to order. They may go through these stages in a different sequence.

It might be more helpful, then, to think of these stages as 'sets' of emotions which we shall experience in our own way and time. We may, too, have to redo one or more emotional stages when different circumstances trigger reactions in us we thought we had left behind. We may be disheartened by going 'two steps forward and one step back', or indeed 'one step forward and two steps back', as it will often seem like this while we are recovering from as traumatic and scarring an event as divorce, but this too is part of any process. It is never a smooth path across the bridge from A to Z. In fact the diagram on the opposite page accurately reflects the up and down nature of our emotions. At all times we are moving, evolving, changing, and—if we allow ourselves to—growing and becoming more independent. It is a process during which, if we observe our reactions, we shall learn about ourselves, our strengths and weaknesses, the systems of behaviour we acquired when we were young. All this comes with the pain and the grieving, and if we have to 'go back and pass go' for the umpteenth time it does not mean failure.

The path which takes us through the landscape of loss can look like this:

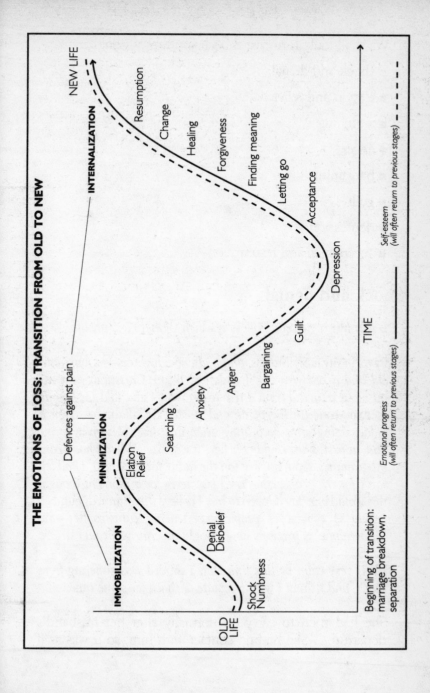

THE EMOTIONS OF LOSS: TRANSITION FROM OLD TO NEW

IMMOBILIZATION

MINIMIZATION

INTERNALIZATION

Defences against pain

NEW LIFE

OLD LIFE

Shock
Numbness

Denial
Disbelief

Elation
Relief

Searching

Anxiety

Anger

Bargaining

Guilt

Depression

Acceptance

Letting go

Finding meaning

Forgiveness

Healing

Change

Resumption

TIME

Beginning of transition: marriage breakdown, separation

Emotional progress
(will often return to previous stages) ——

Self-esteem
(will often return to previous stages) – – –

We shall look in turn at the stages of transition:

- shock and denial
- elation and relief
- searching
- anger
- bargaining
- guilt
- depression
- acceptance and resumption

Shock and denial

It was like a gigantic explosion which shattered... my life.

I was in my early thirties, and had two daughters—a four-year-old and a one-year-old. It was just before Christmas that my husband returned from a trip to Frankfurt and told me he had met someone on the plane and started an affair. I was on a ladder doing some decorating when this news was given to me and, at first, I just couldn't believe it was true. When I had heard programmes about divorce (on the radio, for instance), I had felt sorry for the people concerned but never for a moment thought this would one day happen to me. I believe this stunned, numbed feeling is typical of people experiencing catastrophe—and 'catastrophe' is precisely how I would describe what had struck.

I was very calm by this time, but I think I was suffering from shock, and I think I was in a state of shock for some time.

She had tried to carry on normally after her husband's departure... She had no contact with him, so it was as if he had vanished. She felt numb and very calm.

FROM 'SOLUTIONS', BY TANYA PALMER

These were reactions to very different situations of marital breakdown. The wife in the second quotation was completely unprepared for the trauma of her husband falling in love with, and leaving her for, another woman when they had been married only six years and she had two small children. The shock of this type of situation is devastating, and the world falls in. The numbness experienced by many, the unreality of the situation—living a nightmare and feeling, 'This can't be happening' are our mind's defences against the immediacy of the pain:

I was utterly bewildered. For those three weeks I was completely bewildered... I was completely rocked.

Just as in some circumstances we do not feel the pain of even quite serious *physical* injuries until much later, so we can sometimes block out the awfulness:

■ It's just not true. It can't be happening to me.

■ He'll be back in a day or so when he wants his washing done.

■ She doesn't know what she's doing—this is her home. Perhaps it's her hormones.

■ But it's me he really loves.

When there is a surge of electrical current the fuses overload and blow. In a similar way when there is a sudden pain, too intense to bear, the human body reacts by secreting tranquillizing hormones, which alter our perception of what is happening. This is a survival mechanism in moments of extreme distress which permits the victim to continue functioning rather than going under completely. The stage of shock allows us to marshal some resources to help us cope.

In the immediate aftermath of disaster the person involved may experience a reduced level of feeling and may not react at all. The physical reactions may include any of the following:

- a seeming indifference to what has just happened;

- uncontrollable laughter;

- reduced vision or hearing;

- a sensation of cold or paralysis;

- a sensation of heaviness;

- extreme fatigue.

Sometimes the immediate shock of knowing that this is the end of the marriage prohibits even talking about it. However, it is almost invariably true that we act out what we cannot speak, and not infrequently our bodies will show signs of trauma: we may not be able to eat; we may vomit or have diarrhoea, or need to pass water frequently; some people come out in a rash, and in extreme cases hair can fall out. We may not be able to sleep, going over in our minds again and again the final blow; or sometimes the body will cry out for sleep, and not be able to get enough of it, which gives at least the relief of unconsciousness.

'I don't understand,' we say. 'It was all right really. She was always telling me we never talked but I never dreamed she'd go.' It can take quite a long time for the full impact and the implications of the end of the marriage to hit us. We may have ignored warning signs for many years, and now we cannot face the reality. Shock protects us from having to, until we are more ready to cope.

The shock can immobilize us, or it can sometimes prompt us into desperation, before we have fully understood the consequences:

*I mean... at the start... when I got the letter my first
impression... was probably relating to my cousin [who had
committed suicide]... I'd go for a walk. If I'd had a gun I'd have
gone for a walk and... I was a bit dramatic.*

The methods by which we process (and exclude) information
are geared to defending ourselves from knowledge which is too
painful, to protecting our self-esteem from being blown to
smithereens. If self-esteem is completely destroyed we cannot
function.

This denial can take many forms, and can—in some cases—
be prolonged. In this, more unhealthy, manifestation it can
show itself in some of the following ways:

- attempts to block out everything that recalls the partner
  who has caused the hurt;

- throwing ourself into occupations to avoid thinking about
  the 'lost' partner;

- replacing the 'lost' partner with another too soon;

- making 'shrines' out of places, things and memories;

- using alcohol, drugs or medication as an anaesthetic.

Denial is like armour which both protects us from pain and
from other people's observation of our pain. It is well known
that Queen Victoria's mourning of Prince Albert, with the
shrines and mausoleums she created to 'keep' him alive, was
excessive and bordered on the pathological, but if this phase is
not prolonged it can be helpful. Elisabeth Kübler-Ross[1] writes of
patients who have just learned they will die soon:

I regard it as a healthy way of dealing with the
uncomfortable and painful situation with which some of
these patients have to live for a long time. Denial functions
as a buffer after unexpected shocking news, allows the

patient to collect himself and, with time, mobilize other, less radical defenses... Denial is usually a temporary defense and will soon be replaced by partial acceptance.

Cognitively we do not wish to recognize the reality of what has happened; emotionally we reject the suffering that results from it.

The spouse who has caused this shock by leaving or by deciding that the relationship is past saving may operate their own form of denial, which may be a defence against guilt and remorse. A solicitor[2] writes:

If you have a new partner, you may want to deal with the breakdown by perhaps not dealing with it at all. You want to be free to pursue and develop your new relationships. You do not want to be burdened by wild accusations and emotional blackmail by your spouse. You want to be able to see the children and enjoy time with them. You may want to introduce them to your new partner without feeling that you will be criticized for whatever you do.

The 'leaving' spouse may for this reason also minimize the damage they have done:

She will be fine. After all, she knew I was not happy, that I felt restless, that I had regretted making such a commitment so young. And it isn't as if she hadn't had her moments. Several of them really, in the thirty years... she could have had her fun. I wouldn't have minded much... She's got plenty of friends; she's good at making them and has quite a decent little face, so she will probably find herself someone any day now.

Denial, for both parties, allows us to block out the implications of what has happened. If our hearts refuse to suffer, we protect our battered self-esteem from further diminution.

Elation and relief

> She makes plans and promises a whole new world of work and play.
>
> FROM A SHORT STORY BY TANYA PALMER

This is generally a short-lived phase, if we experience it at all, and may in some cases be an extension of denial. We are still unable to face the enormity of the consequences—emotional, psychological, material, practical—of the ending of our marriage. It may delude those who observe us, and feel responsible for our well-being, that we are already 'over' the pain, whereas in fact we have not yet begun to enter into it.

The delusion can extend to self-justification on the part of the one who is leaving:

> *She goes on about my treachery, but she doesn't seem to see that we only have one life, and not all of us are here much past middle age and if I don't take this opportunity I may never even get to understand what I might be missing. She's got plenty of friends…*

In the terminology of Thomas Harris' book on transactional analysis, this is a false perception of 'I'm OK—you're OK'.

There can be an immense sense of relief that the daily destruction of rows is over; that we have freedom to come and go as we please, without being answerable to anyone; that we can be ourselves without the killing chill of fear of violence; that the loneliness of living with someone who no longer loves and respects us is no more a continuous affront; that the suspicion of our partner's adultery no more erodes our dignity as a person and as a spouse. It may be that there is elation at no more deception and lies, no more pretence, no more emotional blackmail:

> *I got sick of her always wanting to know where I was, and who*

I was with. In any case she was so gullible, swallowed most of my stories even when we had had that big showdown…

We are free; free to be ourselves once more. Despite the hurt, we see new vistas of possibility opening in front of us:

It is my intention to begin life anew as a new kind of person. I am also hoping to make some progress as a writer… there is some satisfaction in having made the break.

In this brief period of exultation in the potential of a future, single (or re-partnered) life, and relief at last at being liberated from the relationship and person that assassinated our self-esteem, we can be temporarily high and we feel able to strike out confidently with the marriage behind us. Unfortunately, although there will be those who conserve this sense of relief, this emotion usually means we have not yet started to mourn:

At the beginning I felt elation, relief, that I had the piece of paper which I never thought I would have. Then totally bereft…

Searching

The following quotation is part of an autobiographical account of how a wife, left by her husband of thirty years after a slowly crumbling relationship during which he had had several affairs, understands how far apart they had gradually moved emotionally. She describes (in the third person) her realization:

She suddenly realized just how much her husband had moved from her. It was more than just leaving the house, leaving the bed and the partnership.

FROM A SHORT STORY BY TANYA PALMER

Any positive feeling of freedom is usually short-lived, and a way—however valid and positive the feelings may be—of coping with the immediacy of pain or solitude once it has hit us:

I decided to make as much contact as possible to prove I loved her.

Bowlby[3], writing about mourning (after a death) in adult life, tells us that the bereaved person will often feel an urge to search for and recover the lost person. Divorce is not dissimilar: the one left behind 'searches', maybe listening for the sound of the car in the drive, the key in the lock. In Tanya Palmer's stories and poems about her experience of divorce, she verbalizes her search by projecting it on to the person of her ex-husband:

But there is no way you can do this, after making your bid for independence. You can't suddenly turn up on the doorstep, clutching a bottle, and say 'Let's have a quiet evening, with you making me something nice to eat, and me telling you about this painting I was doing today.' No, because she might interpret that as you saying 'It's all been a terrible mistake, darling, can I come back?'

The forms of this 'searching', again in many ways a refusal to process accurately the information that the marriage is over, are varied. Bowlby details some: a restless moving about and scanning—visiting old haunts or places where the spouse might be found; thinking intensely about the 'lost' spouse; constantly responding to stimuli (e.g. noises) that suggest the presence of the other and a refusal to pay attention to those considered irrelevant to this aim; and calling for the lost person.

There are sadder, more bitter forms of 'searching': men or women will hang around outside the home of their former partner, hoping to catch a glimpse of them, hoping for a word, a look, as though any contact will provoke a return to normality, and bring the erring one back to the fold. One woman rang her ex-husband's number day and night. She rang her grown-up daughters, her sister, her brother-in-law, her friends, her husband's new lover at all hours in the hope of finding him there—only to tell him (regularly) that there was a problem with her tropical fish tank, and to beg him to come and fix it. These 'searching' ploys went on for two or three years.

Writing on marital breakup, Bowlby[4] notes:

Behaviour influenced by an expectation of ultimate reunion is observed in many women with a husband who has deserted or whose marriage has ended in divorce. Marsden (1969) studied eighty such women, all with children, and dependent on the State for support, a great number of whom had not lived with their husband for five years or more. Remarking on the striking resemblance of the responses shown by some of them to responses seen after a bereavement, Marsden writes: 'The mother's emotional bonds with the father did not snap cleanly with the parting. Almost half the mothers, many of whom had completely lost touch with the father, had a sense of longing for him... *It was evident that a sizable minority of women persisted, in spite of the evidence to the contrary and sometimes for many years, in thinking they would somehow be reunited with their children's father.'* [my emphasis] After having moved into a new house three years earlier one of them had still not unpacked her belongings, unable to believe that the move was permanent.

Anxiety

Mingled with yearning and search at this stage there can be a glimpse of reality, and the future looks scary. This can provoke acute anxiety which often has a practical expression:

- What shall I do for money?
- Who's going to get the children?
- What about the pension/the car/the house?
- Shall I have to go to court?

Anger

When we come to realize that the break is final and that our 'search' is fruitless, fury can follow:

- How dare she?
- He has no right!
- I'll get even with her!

The anger that explodes can be all-devouring, full of spite, bitterness, venom and vengeance. We can lose our reason and almost our sanity in this burning hatred:

I hate him. He's a very wicked person. I hate him; he's so wicked.

A seemingly small incident can bring the realization that love has turned to hate. Maggie's husband walked out one afternoon to live with a young colleague. She says:

He wasn't there when the dog died. I think that was really when hate started to form. I thought 'Any man who can allow his wife and children to take a dog to the vet, have it put down and bring it back and bury it in the garden cannot be worth worrying about.' So I really hated him that night.

Thoughts of vengeance, destruction and harm obsess us, and rare it is that in the fullness of grief we can maintain a giving and generous love towards the person who shared our bed, our home and who is parent to our children. Abigail's detachment is unusual:

At the time I went through a maelstrom of emotions ranging from anger, thoughts of revenge to self-pity, abject misery, self-blame… Despite the anger I sometimes felt (justifiably I thought then, and still do) I did manage to let the better, more forgiving feelings come to the fore and—after eighteen months of trying to hold the marriage together—decided that the best thing would be to get a divorce with the least recrimination possible. I did not want to punish him with an onerous divorce settlement.

There is a normal, understandable and frequent desire to inflict suffering on the cause of our pain, to make them pay the price of their freedom, or to make them come back to heel. Often it is too painful to look at the marriage, and the anger is directed away on to an object who is made to carry all the blame—for example the lover or mistress who seduced our spouse; the interfering parent-in-law who came to live with us (one interviewee said 'Emigrate!' rather than allow relatives to interfere with the couple's life), the lawyers who are trying to screw money out of human misery, the employers who made us redundant and messed up our life, the law's delay, and so on.

'Why?' resounds with fury through the empty spaces of our new life:

- 'Why did you leave?'

- 'Why do you love him more than me?'

- 'Why did you never want to talk about things?'

- 'Why am I not the most important person in your life?'

- 'Why has this happened to me? What have I ever done?'

These questions are less a desire for explanation than a

means of verbalizing anger. Sometimes, if it is still too painful for us to deal with, it is directed at a scapegoat:

- 'Why didn't the marriage guidance counsellor tell her?'

- 'Why didn't the vicar set him right?'

Our anger may well be directed at ourselves for not heeding the warning signs, for not listening to the messages of imminent breakdown, for not agreeing to professional help, for not getting home earlier each night. Even the one who has left for a new relationship can have great bursts of anger and spite:

- 'Why is she making it so difficult for me?'

- 'Why can't I see the children at their bedtime?'

- 'Why is he so demanding?'

- 'Why can't it just be a clean break?'

This is the time when we may send—or receive—letters full of recrimination and hate. We may perpetrate, or be the victim of, acts of spitefulness. Accusations and allegations may fly to and fro. We may refuse to pay household bills, the mortgage, maintenance, the solicitor, and—worst—we may use the children to get back at our former partner.

Yet even anger, if it continues, is a sign that some remnant of hope of regaining time past lingers on. Bowlby[5] tells us that when mother and small child are apart the aggression expressed is to prevent a recurrence of the separation. Between warring adults the effect of aggression will be quite the opposite.

For many people this rage continues for years, and we may stick there, becoming embittered and sour, for acid can erode the vessel which contains it far more than that at which it is thrown. At the time when we most need support and solace from others our attitude may alienate those who might give it to us. We have to try and disentangle the real cause of our fury from the jumble of emotions, and communicate that with accuracy to those around us, rather than going in for the 'kick the cat' syndrome. Those involved with divorcing people should try to remember that there will be real reasons for anger and that these people in their pain are all too often deflecting it away from themselves and on to others. We can help by respecting and understanding this, and gently—when the time is right—helping them address it.

Bargaining

If we have been unable to face reality in the first stage of the loss of the marriage, and have been angry with ourselves and others, then we may try to change things by bargaining. It is a last-ditch attempt to regain what we have lost:

- 'I'll change, I promise, but please come back!'
- 'I'll never see her again, Can we try again?'
- 'I'll do anything, anything…'
- 'I'll give up drinking.'
- 'We'll go for counselling.'

Bargaining occasionally achieves its ends. One man, whose wife had had a well-publicized affair with one of his foreign employees, and who was on the verge of divorce, offered to buy her—for a quarter of a million pounds—the old farmhouse and land where she had grown up. In his case, this bargain was 'successful' in the short term; they attempted to patch up the marriage, and her lover went back to his home country.

Though the errant spouse may return, bargaining alone will not usually resolve the problems which caused the marriage to break down. More often bargaining is an extension of our blindness to the facts of the matter. It is a final clutching at rapidly disappearing self-esteem; if this fails, what is left?

Guilt

He was such a good man; look what I've done.

Coming to terms with loss can be seen as a matter of processing information (a brutal way of describing the phases of mourning). In the stage of guilt the pendulum swings as irrationally as when we deny our loss—but in the opposite direction. Now we experience an overpowering and exaggerated sense of our own failure and responsibility for what has happened. We are not 'OK'; our former partner is. We are now the prey of a pack of 'if onlys':

> ... you constantly question yourself as to what you did wrong. I'd love to know. God, maybe I didn't wash the pillowcases properly. I wish I knew what it was.
>
> JULIA CARLING, INTERVIEWED BY ELIZABETH GRICE IN THE *DAILY TELEGRAPH*,
>
> 27 JANUARY, 1997

And we recite our litany of failures constantly to ourselves and to others:

- 'I should have listened to her more.'
- 'I should have controlled my temper.'
- 'I should have been more patient.'
- 'Perhaps if I'd been better in bed...'
- 'I didn't understand her needs.'
- 'I was selfish, unloving...'

We fear the worst because of what we believe we have done: our partner might not survive—they might kill themselves; we have done irreparable harm to our spouse, our children, and so on.

This negativity is the sign that our self-esteem is at a

perilously low ebb; we have faced the truth and magnified it out of proportion and out of all recognition. Guilt is an emotion which is almost impossible to live with. It can drive us to the depths of despair, and for that reason we may be over-concerned with justifying everything that has happened to finish the marriage. We may also rush into another relationship in order to 'prove' ourselves to be good, innocent, caring and capable people:

> *Quite a few people find new relationships before the divorce is through—to prove to themselves they're an OK person. They also want to work out whether they were to blame for the breakup. One man came to a counselling session delighted. 'It wasn't me!' he said.*
>
> COUNSELLOR

Guilt can also be the root of hostility and aggression, which may then—in a vicious spiral of failure—be responsible for the breakdown of any subsequent relationship.

It may be that long years of unhappy marriage have conditioned us to take the 'blame' for whatever is destructive. Our spouse may have been skilled at loading us with reproach and if we are people whose self-image has never been strong or positive, we shall have accepted this state of affairs and made it a part of ourselves. We are, we feel, worthless and we deserve what has happened.

> *I would have done anything... I've realized my mistakes—I had insecurities. I talked to him about them and wore him down. I'm not capable of being a partner because I've got so much 'baggage'.*

If this is how we feel, then divorce and professional counselling help can be the springboard to change and growth. Now is the time when we need a good friend, therapy, support, a listening ear and acceptance. A non-judgmental, caring and impartial person can help us discern what legitimately we should carry and resolve in terms of responsibility, and can also enable us to distinguish this from an unproductive, negative—and ultimately (if it is prolonged) egocentric—guilt trip.

Depression

I had depression. I thought I was going mad. I've nearly gone mental going over and over what happened.

I had depression after the divorce—it affected my work, and then I had psychiatric treatment, but I stopped the treatment—I didn't want medication.

I took anti-depressants for about three months after the separation. It was common-or-garden depression.

I took Prozac for a while afterwards. I needed support and I was depressed.

There was depression after the divorce.

I took anti-depressants for six months during the divorce.

My mental state went from bad to worse. I could not talk. I thought I was going to collapse in the middle of the high street. I found my way to a surgery, but it was closed so they sent me to the hospital. I just cried. I was referred to this person who I believe was a psychotherapist. I suppose it was a nervous breakdown, yet I didn't know it at the time.

Anger turned in against ourselves can engender a state of despondency, depression or despair, as can the sort of guilty interior monologue described above. We are now 'not OK'. We feel tired and cast down, and in turn we blame ourselves for our inability to rise above these feelings. In extreme forms we may need psychiatric treatment. We have understood: the break is final; no miracle eleventh-hour reprieve is going to happen. We remember and are fully conscious of what we have lost—partner, status, security, role, home, children.

Pain and loss she had anticipated. Not the overwhelming sense of dislocation she was now experiencing, though. She was amazed to discover that her own existence, her own very sense of having a right to be alive was suddenly called into question. For if he did not want her, he who had stood at her side so many years ago and had made promises, who had observed her giving birth, her moments of sexual pleasure, her anxieties and special preoccupations. If he did not want her, why should she be here?

It was not a matter of logic. Her own intelligence recognized that to question her own humanity along these lines was wrong, and yet emotionally these were the thoughts that persisted. Every moment of insecurity magnified itself and was woven together with all the unresolved material of her subconscious to form an accusation of worthlessness. Her dressing-table mirror sneered at her daily, her friends seemed to slip quietly out of reach, her children became wary of hearing her voice on the phone, unwilling to be asked once more to contemplate her sadness.

That picture drawn from the short story called 'Subjective View' by Tanya Palmer, paints a powerful portrait of the disabling lack of self-esteem suffered by a newly-divorced woman, and of the loss of status, identity, the perception of stigma, of feeling an embarrassment and a drag to others.

Almost everybody interviewed during the course of research for this book experienced depression for a significant length of time. When we go through this, the pain is deep and intense and seemingly permanent, and our practical circumstances can exacerbate it. We have to adjust to life without the support of our partner, and yet we may have to be solely responsible for the care and upkeep of young or teenage children when all we want to do is hide under the bedclothes all day. We may have to get up and drag ourselves to work, where—paradoxically—because we are usefully occupied, and there may be camaraderie and support, our self-esteem may receive a short daily boost.

Many people, overwhelmed by the loss of partner, of their previous life and of self will bump along the bottom for months or years, stuck in this slough of despond:

I didn't realize I was depressed. Recovery was not a matter of months... I didn't realize the months were actually years.

One response to it is never to trust again, and to sustain an exaggerated desire for isolation from intimate relationship for we are too vulnerable in our woundedness:

Divorce has completely transformed my outlook on human relations. It has cracked my idealistic outlook.

But paradoxically within that we still feel keenly our deprivation:

I do miss being cuddled.

In the arms of a member of the opposite sex we are comforted and find a fleeting affirmation of our existence.

However, depression is the bottom; it is the pits of loss, and the way is up from now on if and when we permit ourselves to let go of the tragedy that has befallen us, learn from it, and move on:

The fundamental crisis... arises not just from loss of another, but also from loss of self. Familiar thoughts and behaviour no longer make sense. Thus the later stages of mourning involve rebuilding identity and finding new reasons for living. Sadness and depression replace the numbness and anger characteristic of the earlier stages, as the loss is taken on board and people begin the long journey back to participating in a life which has fundamentally changed. The work of grieving will continue until this adjustment is complete.[6]

Perhaps for some a further cause for depression to be added to the multiple loss of structure and meaning in life is the loss of their faith in God, who has turned out for them to be some sort of cosmic sadist, directing all his venom in their direction.

We are ready to let go and move on when we understand that our depression is not caused by the other, but is within ourselves:

> I've suffered from depression, too, and know that it is inherent in one's natural make-up, mental and perhaps genetic. Unhappy experiences can trigger attacks, or exacerbate moods, but basically the problem lies within oneself—it would be most unfair to blame anyone else.

Nevertheless, although we cannot blame the other, the breakup of an intimate relationship can cause a reactive depression which is a normal consequence and which can be long-lasting.

Acceptance and resumption

Gradually, acceptance of our new state liberates us into new ways of feeling, reacting and thinking. This in turn promotes new ways of behaving. We are beginning to be detached. We know we are letting go when we dismantle the shrines we erected to our past life and love, when we can take down the photos and put them in an album, or clear out or send back (rather than tear up or burn) belongings that have been left. It is still not painless , for letting go of the proofs of past happiness is never easy. We are calmer in our dealings, if we have them, with our former partner, and what used to be issues of prime importance now seem no longer to be so. We have coped with so much we could not have dreamed of doing, and have made huge adjustments, both emotional and practical. But doing this has given us a more realistic understanding of what our loss is, and how it can help us be stronger and more autonomous— ultimately more fulfilled—adults:

> I can organize getting my car repaired, paying the bills, summon a plumber—he'd always done that. I can sleep alone in the house. I can run my life.

Searching for meaning

The need to find a meaning to our pain is one sign that we are coming alive again, and it is only at this stage that any real change within ourselves will be possible. Many of the research interviewees said they agreed to answer questions in order to find some meaning to what they had gone through, and to help others do the same:

> Even at sixty-eight I feel I have a lot to offer on my experience. I took the time to think the various processes through and thankfully now I have 'picked up the pieces', and have found a new life.

When we start to ask the following questions of ourselves, we are emerging towards the light:

■ What meaning and use can this pain have in my life?

- How will it help me to know myself better?
- What new resources am I discovering in myself?
- What have I learned?
- What new direction is my life taking?
- How can I develop as a person from now on?

The answers to these questions will not come immediately, sometimes only in retrospect years later, and sometimes not at all. But it is the asking that is more important.

After my marriage failed I understood how dependent I had been on my wife as a mother to me and that my expectations of her were absolutely impossible. Now I have sought professional help and know myself better, and I believe I am becoming more independent as a human being.

I've become a stronger person since I've been on my own. I think I lived in his shadow rather. It's made me see things through different eyes. He was a controlling personality and he used to make me feel guilty.

Letting go after a divorce is, almost everyone will say, far harder than saying goodbye finally to a dead partner, for our former husband or wife is alive, possibly living not far away with a new lover or spouse, and we must necessarily meet, telephone, see each other when the children visit:

Years later, when I had a friend who had been widowed, I was to feel privately that I would have had a much easier time if my husband had died suddenly. All the wonderful memories would have been preserved, there would have been no guilty feelings or need to attribute blame, and there would have been much more sympathy and support from other people.

Many will never quite loosen their emotional ties, and if so we feel resentful about the clichés of letting go, moving on better, stronger and wiser people:

I wish I could say something upbeat and encouraging about 'working through to become a stronger and wiser person' to use all the clichés. Unfortunately, I can't, in all honesty.

We shall often need to redo some or all of the sets of emotions while mourning our marriage—again and again—before we have finally said goodbye to it. It is never a simple progression, and to let go completely is rare. Events and crises will cause us to regress, and some scars will remain. There will always be sensitive, tender places, and wounds which will reopen easily, perhaps especially when we come to a new relationship and encounter difficulties in that. Nevertheless, we can take comfort in remembering that scar tissue is tougher than the rest.

The process of divorce, when all these aspects are taken into consideration, leaves men and women (and their children) highly vulnerable. It is a time when we need all the support we can get, but ironically it is just at this time we are most likely to feel most isolated socially. It is not just that social life may be a problem (or an impossibility if we are tied by small children and lack of money, or are too depressed to go out), but friends and family may be less than supportive and may even turn away from us. We discuss the social dimension of divorce in the next chapter.

1. Elisabeth Kübler-Ross, *On Death and Dying*, Routledge, 1995 © Elisabeth Kübler-Ross 1969.
2. Simone E. Katzenberg, *The Seven Stages of Divorce*, Solomon Taylor and Shaw, 1996.
3. John Bowlby: *Attachment and Loss Volume 1: Attachment,Attachment and Loss Volume 2: Separation: Anger and Anxiety*; *Attachment and Loss: Volume 3: Loss: Sadness and Depression*, Penguin Books, © The Tavistock Institute of Human Relations, 1980.
4. John Bowlby, *Loss*, (*see above*), Penguin Books, 1991, page 90.
5. John Bowlby (*see note 4*), page 91.
6. Christopher Clulow and Janet Mattinson, *Marriage Inside Out: Understanding the Problems of Intimacy*, Pelican Books, © The Tavistock Institute of Medical Psychology, 1989.

7

The social dimension

'Look, you know I go to the Red Lion. Couldn't you go to the Queen's Head or any other pub? I can't bear it when I walk in and you're there. Everyone stops; they don't know what to say or do. I've lost everything: I've lost you; I've lost the house, the home. I've lost all my friends and my freedom. I cannot really go round to friends in case you're there. I don't know how to handle it. I don't know if I walk into that pub whether you're going to be there or not.'

That was Mandy's plea to her ex-husband who, after their divorce, had moved away from the village where they lived, and then returned eighteen months later. Mandy was distraught at this unexpected twist of the knife.

One happily married husband and wife, close friends of a warring couple who subsequently divorced, continued to see the former husband regularly and invited him for meals once he was on his own. This act of kindness was deeply resented by the former wife, who then refused to have anything to do with her friends. She felt they had betrayed her, and—as she saw it—had 'sided with' her ex-husband.

The social dimension of divorce is one that is rarely given the consideration that perhaps it merits. Not unnaturally, we tend to concentrate on our feelings about the relationship, the children and other practical matters. The social consequences, however, are not always easy to cope with.

The public and the private

Divorce changes your relationship to everything—the milkman, people in the shops, everyone…

Divorce is a wave which goes out and affects other people.
COUNSELLOR

One of the central (and perhaps few) distinctions between marriage and cohabitation is the willingness of the man and woman to make a lifelong *and public* commitment to each other and to the relationship. Marriage implies that the couple have both a place and a stake in society, and that the unit they are creating together out of two existing units is, while intensely personal and private, also part of the fabric of the wider community, so that they belong both to each other and to the outside world. This evolution, from being a pair with eyes only for each other to being a partnership which is integrated into the social fabric, constitutes a large part of the process which is marriage. In other words, husband and wife are not an island entire unto themselves.

When a marriage breaks down and the couple split up, this rupture harms and diminishes the social environment in which they have lived, moved and had their being. In a microcosmic way, violence is done to the society to which they have belonged. Just as (in theory) the community returns its support when a couple make their marriage vows in public, we can see the converse happen—consciously or not—when the vows are broken and the unit breaks up. Those who people our immediate world and who have known us as a couple may find it more than difficult to relate to us as individuals:

A widely reported experience of re-established single people is the feeling that couples speak an entirely different language. Communicating some single experiences is nearly impossible... Some couples may see you as a threat, or at the very least as setting a dangerous example... The shock, misery and, perhaps, public humiliation of your separation has propelled you into an entirely different universe from that inhabited by couples.[1]

Despite a divorce rate of around 40 per cent, the dissolution of a marriage is somehow still regarded by some people as at best a reprehensible and probably avoidable failure, or at the worst deviant. We all, to a certain extent, have invested in our social landscape, and have an interest in keeping it unchanged. Change is threatening, and those whom we encounter can be uncomfortable if the roles in which they been accustomed to see us are suddenly different:

> ... they found her broken ankle so much easier to cope with than her broken marriage
>
> FROM 'SOLUTIONS' BY TANYA PALMER

Fear of the divorced

Often the people least likely to get asked to social events are those recently bereaved or divorced. The rest of the world fears our pain, afraid (no doubt unconsciously) that it will flow out of us and engulf the gathering. They are afraid we shall talk embarrassingly of it. There may be some justification for this, as those in the grips of loss often tend to suffer from logorrhoea (more commonly, and unkindly, known as verbal diarrhoea), and seem compelled to talk about themselves and what they have lost:

> Her friends seemed to slip quietly out of reach; her children became wary of hearing her voice on the phone, unwilling to be asked once more to contemplate her

sadness. Her elderly parents handled the difficult subject of her divorce by not referring to it... She is beset with the need to make others feel comfortable in her presence.

FROM 'SUBJECTIVE VIEW' BY TANYA PALMER

Even today, when there are greater numbers of divorced and separated men and women around than ever before, there is a tendency to regard divorcees as sexual predators:

The female divorcee, like her male counterpart, was seen as sexually aggressive and younger women, especially, found themselves having to fend off the unwanted advances of male neighbours, casual dates and even the local roundsmen. This 'easy game' stereotype was matched for men by the label 'wolf'. The male divorcee could not be trusted alone with women and, if separation was accompanied by a loss of friends, the male often attributed his rejection to that cause.[2]

Stigma

Blame and opprobrium often remain the lot of those whose marriages have ended, despite thirty or so years of the 'permissive society', a high rate of marital breakup, the example of so many celebrity and royal divorces, and even a softening on the part of some of the churches. Some sort of stigma is still attached to those whose marriages fail, and even today the paradox is occasionally seen of divorced people who would not themselves wish to marry another divorcee:

The public has sympathy for a widow, pity. There is none of that for a divorced woman.

I would have had a much easier time if my husband had died suddenly... there would have been much more sympathy and support from other people.

Those in the couple's social network will generally have only an outsider's view of the relationship, and may be confused or downright judgmental:

Other people, including family and friends, didn't view things in quite such a serious light.

If they talk to one partner they may feel acutely disloyal to the other. To shift uncomfortable feelings outside oneself and project them on to another is a human reaction to such a situation, and so—because of their discomfiture—outsiders may blame and shun one or both former partners, or unjustly take sides:

My ex-wife [was] going around the collective friends of thirty years' standing, and damning me. Consequently, a large number of friends vanished, save for the few who wanted to know my side too. That was one of the worst happenings, but I understand that it is an accepted pattern.

Unkind and cruel gossip may now also be a feature of the divorcee's life. The two divorcing people will be forced (as Mandy was trying above) to disentangle their social networks, with the loss of relationships with friends that this will inevitably entail.

Once again, it is perhaps the older divorcee who suffers most from feelings of stigma and discredit, though these may not necessarily be founded. Those who married in or before the middle years of the twentieth century were committed, generally speaking, more than are subsequent generations (for whom it may still be the ideal), to the vow of marriage 'till death do us part'. There may be few or none in their immediate circle who have personal experience of the trauma of divorce, and so they may be regarded as freaks, and shunned.

Those who are divorcing may feel they have let down those close to them and, by extension, society itself:

I would have divorced him very early on if my parents had not been so violently opposed to the marriage in the first place. I felt I was letting everybody down

I felt an obligation to all the people in my life to try and make the best of things.

I just thank God my parents died before all this.

Those who have a religious faith, or who are members of a church, may find that the social interactions that can result from these may provide not only friendship and perhaps useful activity, but maybe solace and spiritual comfort too. But at just the time when these blessings are most needed the divorced individual may also find the most bruising attitudes. We examine the spiritual implications of divorce in Chapter 10.

Loss of social circle

When our marriage has broken up it can seem that everyone else is happily married (though this manifestly cannot be true), and that we are the odd one out, the failure, the one who was not good enough—or even the wicked seducer. We do not always want people to know what is going on.

During the initial phase of the breakup of our marriage we may be desperately trying to give the impression that all is well with our relationship, and in order to safeguard this illusion we may even reduce contact with neighbours and friends so these do not find out. We may wish not to be disloyal to our partner and damn them by recounting the awfulness of our current existence, and there may also perhaps be a feeling of loyalty to the relationship, and a need to protect children from teasing by their peers. Or simply we do not want the news to spread because it is too shameful. For this reason, too, close family members may not be informed of trouble in the relationship.

However, the consequence of this, when outsiders do find out, may be bewilderment and hurt on the part of those who considered themselves close to us, and who might have given support, but who now feel rejected or excluded. Many people interviewed said they had lost all their friends because of their divorce, but disclaimed responsiblility for this desertion:

Obviously there is a parting of the ways—his friends and my friends. Some of that is inevitable, but I am thinking of one friend in particular who had been a friend of mine, as was her father before her—before I got married—and I just could not believe it. They even took his side.

When we split up from our partner it is almost inevitable that we shall be cut off from others whom we have known either jointly with, or primarily through, our spouse. Often friends of both partners, not knowing with whom to side, give up the friendship with both rather than remain in this awkward dilemma. Friends from work (if we have a job) may be some of the few remaining social contacts we keep at this painful time.

Probably the worst time of social desertion or discrimination is when we find ourselves for the first time amongst the 'failed'—the separated or the divorced—before we have time to adapt to a new lifestyle, perhaps a new area and our new social identity. It will seem at first that society is based on pairs rather than families or single people. Readjustment and acceptance of our situation will boost our confidence, which in turn promotes and fosters social contacts of varying degrees of depth. However, from time to time an event, a chance remark, a seeming slight will remind us that we no longer conform to what society still considers to be the norm. We may react with hurt, misery, anger or depression and have to go back and relive earlier stages of our grieving process.

New contacts

There are often few enough opportunities for the divorced to make new social contacts, but even these may be compromised by the lack of social confidence that the divorcee may experience. During the years of bringing up children, or working long hours to build up a business we may have lost the knack of meeting new people and forming friendships. Furthermore our self-esteem may have been so diminished by the breakdown of the marriage that we simply do not have the courage or energy to face new situations and people. This is especially true of those who were divorced older, after a longer marriage.

But the onus is squarely on us to go out to other people, for it is unlikely that they will come to us. Making new contacts and fostering these into friendships may require us to change how we think of ourselves, how we view our life, and how we interact with others. This is a departure which can herald a fresh start in life, but for many of us, locked into old patterns of thought and behaviour which often reproduce the systems we acquired from our families of origin, professional help in the form of counselling or therapy may be needed in order to relearn forms of social interaction.

We live in a society which has increasingly permitted divorce, but which has not provided for its consequences. The marital therapists Christopher Clulow and Janet Mattinson[3] say:

The social consequences of divorce have been likened to being despatched to a foreign country where one is confronted by new customs and practices, but without a foreign language or frontier to make it clear that a journey has been made. The lack of social support and ritual for the newly separated can be so great that it drives some into remarriage in order to recover a slot in society.

There is little preparation, minimal support, no structure and no sense of objective unless it is to seek another partner. Some sort of formal transitional rite—as death has funerals to close the chapter—to ease the passage and give social reality to the change of status might help.

The pain of the end of the marriage can only be compounded by the intense loneliness that can often result. Nevertheless, it is virtually axiomatic to say that we 'discover who our true friends are'. Real friends are those who stick by us, and yet can tell us the truth, however painful. They will tell us with honesty what our responsibility may have been in the downfall of the marriage, and will stop us shoving the blame unrealistically and entirely on to our 'ex'. If we persist in doing this we shall live in a cut-off world where we cannot interrelate with others. True friends are enablers in this situation: they listen, accept, tell the truth, and give us the sense of dignity and value which comes from that, and which our marriage may never have provided. Friends will help us through, and—further—help us to reconstruct our lives.

1. Hamish Keith with Dinah Bradley, *Becoming Single*, Pocket Books, 1993. © Hamish Keith, 1991.

2. From the paper by Nicky Hart, 'Contrasts and correspondences in the meaning of marital breakdown for men and women', given to the 1974 Conference of the British Sociological Society on Sexual Divisions and Society, page 19.

3. Christopher Clulow and Janet Mattinson, *Marriage Inside Out: Understanding the Problems of Intimacy*, Pelican Books, © The Tavistock Institute of Medical Psychology, 1989, page 158.

8

The 'leaver' and the 'loser'

*You were my love
and though you left
you held all the keys
to my secret self.
No mystery stirs
to sweeten my life,
I'm simply now
an unwanted wife*

FROM A POEM BY TANYA PALMER

I remember feeling guilt. I felt a shit

In marriage breakdowns where one partner desires divorce and the other does not, there can be a world of difference between how each reacts to and copes with the termination. Divorce is rarely an amicable and clean affair between two equally consenting parties: in practice, one usually *leaves* the relationship and the other *loses* it. The less one spouse wishes to stay, and the more the other clings to the relationship and all that goes with it, the messier and more painful things become for all concerned.

Sarah and Matthew

Sarah and Matthew had been married for five years and had two young children. They came to counselling saying they had made a joint decision to divorce, but the counsellor was left with a strong feeling that Sarah wanted the marriage to end more than Matthew did. Sarah had said at length in the initial counselling session that she didn't feel she had any support in the marriage and that she would be better off alone. She emphasized, however, that she wanted to remain friends with her husband for the sake of the children.

Once couples are in the hands of solicitors any intended amicable settlement can become adversarial, and one of the spouses can naturally slip into the role of the aggrieved and abandoned partner. The new divorce legislation aims to reduce this confrontational entrenchment.

We have begun to see that when marital breakup happens the losses to be grieved, accepted and internalized are complex and multi-faceted. Even when we are no longer in love with our partner we may still be attached to our role as husband or wife, which may perhaps incorporate a parental role as well which could disappear with a custody ruling. We may still need the status of being married for our own feelings of self-worth, as the secure base, as the resource which helps us to carry on with our other tasks and roles (for example, at work). In other words, the relationship may have retained value for us, even though we cannot maintain harmony with our partner. We may of course still love our spouse, but recognize that the relationship is not viable (it may have been spoiled by infidelity or other behaviours which compromise its essence). All these aspects of marriage may therefore be lost, against our will, when our partner decides to terminate it.

The one who requests the cessation of the married relationship has initially a certain measure of control over what happens, and this may put them in a position of power. They have more time mentally and often practically to prepare for life beyond marriage, can perhaps envisage new roles to replace those relinquished or lost, and so in many ways conserve their self-image at a level which is acceptable and which permits them to function. The partner who is left, whose pattern of existence has been smashed and destroyed for ever, may be unable, because of shock or depression, to formulate plans which will help them regain some self-respect.

Often the one left behind has little or no time to prepare themselves for this trauma, to adjust to the reality of what has happened. They will be forced in the most brutal way to begin mourning their loss, and to start on that journey, which may never end, of coming to terms with it. In the course of research for this book the scenario was described time and again of one partner coming home to find a note on the table or the mantelpiece, or a solicitor's letter through the post, which was *to them* the first intimation of trouble:

I thought he was lying at the bottom of the Thames. Then I heard he'd gone on holiday with her.

To the leaver it represented either the final straw, or a planned escape.

The leaver may of course say, and maybe with some truth, that their partner had been warned, given ultimata, even threatened with this rupture, but yet took no notice. Nevertheless, the blow is none the softer for hearing, 'I warned you this would happen but you wouldn't listen/change.' The initiation of divorce proceedings, as we have seen, can arise out of a desperate bid for help, for communication, for affection, to be taken notice of. If these are not forthcoming, our bluff has been called.

The amount of warning we receive of such a blow will greatly influence how prepared we are for this transition. It also determines whether we can retain any sense of control over what is happening to us, and from it the potential for restructuring—and this is vital for self-esteem.

She got in our car with our two boys after kissing me goodbye; she was to visit my parents in Oxford. We were then to meet in the Cotswolds… she simply never came back. Her abrupt, unlooked for, unexpected departure an arrow to my heart. Divorce smashed through the hymen of my reserve... it destabilized me for a while.

This is why mediation (see Appendix 1) can be so helpful and—ultimately—healing for the one left behind, for it gives them the opportunity to state their needs, and for these to be heard impartially so they may form the basis of an agreement on the future, even if that is to be apart.

But when we are faced with shock and loss all in one, the crisis of transition can become a drama. The danger scenario will contain one or more of these elements:

- It comes out of the blue.

- It is sudden.

- We are powerless to change events.

- It entails loss of role and status.

- There is no accepted ritual or rite of passage to mark the ending.

Divorce is not just a reversal of getting married, for usually when we wed it is the crowning of a period of courtship, a process of creating bonds and links which are then solemnized in matrimony. But we cannot assume that divorce for *both* parties is always the culmination of a gradual and progressive untying of conjugal knots. As we have seen, one partner may be entirely blind to all warning signs and be genuinely thunderstruck when the solicitor's letter arrives or their spouse leaves.

We tend to assume that the final decree follows a prolonged period of disenchantment, growing apart, unhappiness with the spouse role, and breakdown of marital routines. However, the culture does not provide any scripts for dissolving marital bonds. Furthermore, while the creation of such bonds is a joint effort, the breakup of them is typically initiated by one partner only. For the other partner, this sets in motion a set of changes which are involuntary. To make it even more difficult for the person who is facing role loss because of the other's decision to exit, there is often little opportunity to create transitional time.[1]

The leaver *exits* from their role as spouse, whereas the one left *loses* theirs whether they will or not, and this is one of the vital differences.

The leaver

Even if you're the one that's leaving, it still knocks you about.
COUNSELLOR

The leaver is often able to go through the sequence of changes necessary to become psychologically and physically 'not married' at a pace which they dictate and control. These changes reverse all that makes up the union, and imply emotional disengagement and withdrawal, extrication from everyday routines, and cutting through the shared experiences and projects and interdependence that are the 'glue' of the relationship. The leaver may appear to emerge unscathed because they:

- have already undergone some of the stages of coming to terms with loss;

- may well have bidden farewell to guilt and depression (if they ever experienced them) before divorce becomes a reality;

- may refuse to look at their emotions at all.

I thought she'd get over it. She's had worse before really and survived. I thought in a year or so we'd all be able to have dinner together.

Leavers can establish for themselves networks of support and sympathy which will encourage and vindicate them, and boost their self-esteem. They may well themselves already be in another relationship, and if it is a recent one most probably still be insulated within the stage of romance and high-octane passion.

Denial

Often the pain and guilt of what we are doing is so great that we repress it, bury it and refuse to deal with it, giving the impression that we have done nothing of significance.

Guilt and failure

The leaver is not always exempt from feelings of guilt, shame, self-doubt, failure and diminished self-esteem, and the temptation will then be—if it has not already happened—to boost the self-image with a quick emotional fix with a third party, not necessarily a lover, but a friend or family member who will feed the self-justification that helps us feel better. One man, in the midst of protracted divorce proceedings, rapidly acquired a new girlfriend, but told her:

Wherever I go till the end of my days I shall drag round my guilt and my doubt, and you can cry all the tears in the world, I shall still wonder whether I've done the right thing.

The one who walks out, or extricates themselves from the marriage, does not necessarily—contrary to the beliefs of many 'left' spouses—find life easy:

*Ten years after, I still lie awake at night wondering if it was right.
What I have is an overwhelming sense of failure, even though I
could not have stayed with her. I also now question my judgment,
because I got things so wrong and I chose the wrong woman even
though my heart was telling me I'd made a mistake.*

Fear

Alongside this sense of failure is the fear of the consequences of
the marital breakup. We may fear that our partner is really not
capable of spending time on their own, let alone cope with the
practical things we have done for them for so many years:

> Sometimes a partner who is planning to leave a marriage
> will suggest seeking help for the relationship as a means of
> ensuring that there will be someone to pick up the pieces
> when he or she leaves. Occasionally there are good reasons
> for questioning a partner's ability to manage alone. Quite
> often, however, the instigator is looking for help with
> feelings of guilt about leaving or locating in their partner
> fears about their own viability after breakup.[2]

We may also harbour a fear that our former spouse may try
to commit suicide. Indeed, they may have threatened to in an
attempt to coerce us into staying. People will often take their
own lives in order to:

- take revenge on the one who has deserted them;

- destroy their self to erase their overpowering sense of
guilt;

- end a life which is no longer worth living without a
loving relationship.

Attempted suicide or self-destructive gestures are often
provoked by:

- a desire to punish the attachment figure and gain more attention;

- the 'cry for help' to the attachment figure who is seen as neglectful.[3]

A clean break...

Despite these fears—conscious or not, justified or not—that the one left will not survive, the leaver will often not make their intentions clear—hence the frequent reliance on notes left on mantelpieces and suchlike. Once the decision has been truly taken, and the leaver is certain they cannot stay in the relationship, for whatever reason, then they must be definite and say what they are going to do:

> I had a sense of having done something outrageous. I told Barbara what I had done, and then we slung the camping gear into the car and went off to walk for a few days till we'd talked it through. We talked ourselves through to the point where we'd try and make it [Barbara's acceptance of his new relationship] work. I thought this would free Barbara up to go her own way.

If they are sure they have to leave, then they must not be dissuaded by the attempts of the spouse to make them feel guilty and wicked, by tears, aggression, violence, pleas and threats. The leaver must communicate that trying 'one more time' is not on, and that the process of mourning has begun.

Among the different experiences between 'leaver' and 'loser' is the fact that it is the one who takes the initiative in divorce who is more likely to leave the family home, often to set up in another household with another person. The leaver, or partner active in the breakup is also more likely to remarry—partly because there may already be a new partner, or because they are less crushed by lack of self-esteem, and thus emotionally more resilient.

The loser

Those left, especially those who had little or no warning of impending breakdown, will—as we have seen—experience chaos in their lives as the fabric of their marriages unravels before their eyes. Familiarity, routine, structure go at a stroke, and the status of spouse with them. They will perhaps have had no time to negotiate, to repair, or to build the supports round them which they will need so desperately during this time. Maybe they do not know how to do these things. The 'losers' will have feelings, often acute, of failure, of personal powerlessness, and will experience disarray in their lives on every level. Often they will make superhuman efforts to control some area of their life, to prove they are in charge of events:

> *I gave up smoking right in the middle of the worst part. That's my willpower. I stopped.*

The grief is a multiple one, depriving the loser in almost every area of life. And in the face of such bereavement and such deprivation it will take all we have got sometimes merely to survive: there is little energy or taste for those areas which we have *not* lost (these may include children and work, both of which can suffer from neglect or incapacity at this time—and for many months or years to come).

Denial

Most of us do not plan to divorce; it does not fit into the scheme of things when we project into the future. When we do marry we make heavy investments in being a husband or wife. If the marriage ends, our role identity takes a beating. Because of the strength and intensity of our feelings of guilt, shame, failure, defeat and rejection we may be unwilling to accept that the end of the marriage has come. When all the facts are pointing to a closed door we may yet cling on to the belief that the relationship can still work, and we may be unwilling for other people to know our circumstances, since their knowledge of our situation gives it a sort of objective reality. The passive partner in a marriage breakup may even withdraw from social interaction outside the home in order to be able to control the flow of information.

Losses

Role, status and structure

Gone are order, control and predictability. Gone is the role of spouse, which may have been a key part of the person's identity, especially if they have spent many years sacrificing their own identity to that of their partner (as 'homemaker' perhaps, or even more acutely when their life has been lived through and for the other—for example, a vicar's or diplomat's wife/husband). Gone (for women) may be a cherished legal status. Gone are the routines of everyday life, the comfort in established habits and shared language. And often gone, too, is the home with its familiarity and security. When these all disappear, self-esteem often goes with them, and the bottom falls out of the world. Those left will often go to extreme lengths (pleading with the leaving spouse, using the children as go-betweens or as levers, threatening suicide or violence, starting new relationships immediately) to regain what has been lost.

Partner—love—sex

> As your running runs out
> Passed kyros' trusts no prayer
> Nothing anymore chok'd back in
> Never was there a last kiss,
> Or wave-down valley of the shadow
> High-Low-way of half-life-light
> In goodbye cariad like this
>
> FROM A POEM, MALE DIVORCEE[4]

And then—over and above the loss of the marriage, and the role, status and structure which marriage confers—there is the loss of the person in whom we have invested our emotional energy and our very self, for perhaps half a lifetime. We may feel that we no longer have worth in that person's eyes, and our identity crumbles. With the end of the marriage, sexual contact and release, if they survived thus far, disappear.

For the partner who is reluctant or unwilling to divorce, any reduction in their circumstances—financial or domestic—will be far more difficult to adapt to than for the one whose ended marriage means a more positive step in a new direction:

> Those who were exposed to an abrupt change of circumstances through no direct action of their own were more resentful of the resulting inconvenience. The woman... whose social status and lifestyle are ruined when her husband leaves her against her will... feels a much greater sense of deprivation than a wife who suffers the same fate but who took deliberate steps to bring about the end of the marriage. The plight of the 'passive' partners was to some extent mitigated by their tendency to retain the marital home.[5]

The rejected 'passive' partner will always suffer more than the active one.

The house as metaphor of the loser

> I move around
> the edges, too;
> the carpet's stains,
> the scuffed and worn,
> the time displaced,
> the home disgraced.

FROM A POEM BY TANYA PALMER

We suggested above how traumatic it can be to have to leave or lose—in addition to the relationship—the familiarity and security of the family home. During the research interviews for this book the house emerged frequently as a metaphor for the person who was suffering from the ending of the marriage. It was as though it was too painful to own the feelings, but they were able to talk about their painful emotion by using the home as an image:

I'm thinking about my abandoned house, and all that happened there—the children, the meals, the lights on in the evening. Now it's deserted and empty and all the furniture has gone. It has been stripped.

We fought over the house. It was the most awful fight. I didn't dare leave it—go out of doors. Then I had to get out—they told me on Christmas Eve. I was totally bereft—it was the loss of the house, I suppose, and all my roots.

When one partner takes a decision to terminate the marriage, or is seriously considering it, the process will usually include an emotional withdrawal from the other and from the relationship. This in turn prompts greater tensions, complaints—and perhaps a desire on the part of the *other* partner to end the relationship. On the other hand the 'left' spouse may go to enormous lengths to make the marriage more viable and attractive to the 'leaver' (the bargaining referred to in Chapter 6). When the 'leaver' has made public their intention of leaving and ending the relationship, the other partner may then give up these attempts, feeling publicly dishonoured, shamed and humilated.

The two partners should, ideally, have talked long before, and the one who is dissatisfied should have communicated accurately the causes of their unhappiness or discontent with the marriage. Leaving a marriage is drastic; it is traumatic for all concerned, and all the options should be explored first. Unfortunately, the tensions and emotional distance in some marriages are so great that it makes exploring these options together (except in the safety of the counselling room or the mediation centre) impossible.

Both the loser and—less obviously—the leaver need to go through some rite of passage, a transitional process of mourning what has been lost—in roles, status, relationship, self-esteem— and the other partner. Put at its simplest, coming to terms with loss means gradually assimilating and accurately processing the information that the marriage is over, and is a gradual transition through stages of emotion. Not only is there a marked difference between leaver and loser in how we are able to do that, but between husband and wife as well.

1. Gunhild O. Hagestad and Michael A. Smyer, 'Patterns of Divorcing in Middle Age', in *Personal Relationships, 4 Dissolving Personal Relationships*, ed. Steve Duck, Academic Press, 1982.
2. Christopher Clulow and Janet Mattinson, *Marriage Inside Out: Understanding the Problems of Intimacy*, Pelican Books, © The Tavistock Institute of Medical Psychology, 1989.
3. John Bowlby *Attachment and Loss: Volume 3: Loss: Sadness and Depression*, Penguin Books, © The Tavistock Institute of Human Relations, 1980.
4. From 'Across the bridge I saw' © David Lloyd-Howells,1986.
5. From the paper by Nicky Hart, 'Contrasts and correspondences in the meaning of marital breakdown for men and women', given to the 1974 Conference of the British Sociological Society on Sexual Divisions and Society.

9

'His' divorce and 'her' divorce

*I (speak) from the vantage point of a woman, but I'm very well
aware, too, of how much divorce, or any breakdown in personal
relationships hurts men.*

FEMALE DIVORCEE

*The male victim is not a fashionable person at the moment… you've
got the emotional damage as well as the financial damage and the
health damage, and all the other problems that come with that.*

MALE DIVORCEE

The difference in perception between the two partners when a
marriage is going down the slope to divorce is accentuated by
the gender difference which makes itself felt in all marriages:

When men and women talk about their marriage there is
always his reality and her reality.[1]

If both spouses are interviewed individually about their
marriage this results in two different accounts, which may
often be highly inconsistent with each other. The
researcher may then try to compare these two narratives
and, rather like a judge, try to determine what the 'story'
of the marriage really is.[2]

- 'You said…'

- 'No, I said…'

- 'No, you didn't.'

- 'I did.'

- 'It wasn't like that.'

- 'You don't remember…'

And so the dance goes on, often long past the formal ending of the marriage—the music ready to start whenever the former couple have any contact with each other.

The dance will have begun when the couple ceased being (if they ever had been) able to communicate accurately to each other their emotions, their hopes, fears and expectations of each other, the relationship and life together. When that happens anger (which often masks other emotions which may not be recognized or acknowledged) can result, and rows follow, and the vicious downward spiral starts. By the time the petition for divorce is filed there are two entirely separate sets of perceptions, remembrances and understanding.

It is not just the reality of one event which is differently interpreted, but the perception of the whole marriage.

Bill and Marion

Bill was a headmaster on the point of retirement. A month or so before he left work he announced his intention of leaving Marion when he retired. He said she had not loved him for many years, and that he had never been able to please her. Marion did not want to end the marriage and considered she had been supportive of Bill and his career. She had no idea of the emotional gap between them that her husband experienced, and their respective image of the marriage had almost nothing in common.

A local GP told the story of a man who came to see him and wept in the surgery. The patient and his wife had been married eighteen years, both actively involved in a business they ran jointly. The husband had often had to be away at weekends for their work, but to him his wife seemed happy with their life.

One night he came back in the early hours after a business trip, to find a note saying: 'Sorry. I've left you.' Her departure had obviously been well prepared for she had taken all her things and had gone to stay with her parents a few miles away. For three months he had no contact with her. He told the doctor that she wanted a divorce on the grounds of 'unreasonable behaviour' because he was so frequently absent. He was perplexed and confused by this, since his times away were for their business, and he had never been unfaithful.

His and hers—nature or nurture?

Research made public in the summer of 1997[3] suggests that there may be genetic reasons why men and women not only perceive social interactions differently but will behave differently in response to certain social and emotional stimuli. These experiments tend to confirm that differences between males and females in social functioning, perception, intuition and language may be more 'nature' rather than 'nurture'—that is, the result of chromosomal constitution and a phenomenon known as 'genomic imprinting', rather than a gender variation in conditioning. It has been suggested that men really do hear conversations differently from women, and that this is indelibly part of their cognitive make-up.

But whether the cause is genetic or acquired, there is a wide gulf between men and women, not only in their perception of the relationship and its breakdown, but also in how they are affected by divorce. The ten-year study by Judith Wallerstein[4] tends to confirm this:

> What emerged very clearly is that, just as at the time of the initial separation, *his* version and *her* version often varied considerably from each other.

This chapter concerns the way the two sexes survive divorce.

144

'His' divorce

For both sexes, divorce can represent the end of the world as they know it, or it can be a release—for some even a happy one. However, unless they are going straight into another committed relationship, men are thought to suffer from the consequences of the divorce to an even greater extent than women, for a variety of reasons, and to cope less well with the losses incurred—loss of partner and perhaps of paternal role, the breakdown of social networks, disruption to career and finances—possibly leading to mental and physical ill-health, and bringing an increased risk of early death.

In general terms, men tend to jump into another relationship more quickly in order to salve their wounds, if they do not already have a new partner at the time of the divorce. It makes things easier, though the temptation is to move from one immature and dependent relationship to another. The psychiatrist and 'marriage doctor', Jack Dominian, apparently ignoring the concept of the 'New Man', said:

> Men have a pattern of wanting to be looked after and seeking that. On the whole they are more dependent than women. If their wives get fed up and chuck them out, or if they walk out, they often go and get someone else on whom to lean.

If they neither find someone, nor resolve their issues of dependency and nurturance, then divorce can be hell for men.

The male mid-life crisis

If men initiate divorce it is often later in the marriage than when women do. The male mid-life crisis (the 'male menopause' or 'andropause', as it is sometimes called) does—according to the many interviewees who ascribed the end of their marriages to it—appear to be more than the popular myth that it is sometimes presented to be. One counsellor said:

> *So often the man really does escape and run off with his secretary. He can say 'Here's someone who will take me as I am.'*

In mid-life a change often occurs in the interests and value systems of individuals. This may be partly because roles change and parenting ceases, as also may 'bread-winning'—the traditional male role. Sometimes men's sexual urges become less imperious and performance less impressive, which can be devastating for those who define themselves by their prowess in that area, and they may need to go out and 'prove themselves'. Their wives, too, may be less welcoming sexually. Or they simply yearn for, and seek, the unshackled potency of their youth. Parents die, and we realize we are next in line. It is frequently a time when a man may become more concerned with interior things—he may stay at home more, look after grandchildren, become fascinated by matters of the mind, spirit or emotions. A woman, on the other hand, may become more interested by external things—she may carve out a new life professionally or in other ways. In a healthy marriage the differences in the other partner will be recognized, accepted and appreciated by the other spouse, and this can breathe new life into a relationship.

But if there is not a solid basis of love and communication between husband and wife, this time may be one of different experimentation, and men, if they do not seek to rediscover lost vigour and sexuality, may simply just want 'out'. Conrad, whom we met in Chapter 5, felt he had no identity of his own at home. He did not communicate any of his feelings to Dana, who was completely taken aback when her husband left. He has now started a new relationship with a younger woman, which seems to be an attempt to discover some sort of personal and sexual identity.

For men the main negative changes that arise from the

breakdown of their marriages are emotional, social, physical and mental, and professional, while positive changes include improved practical and domestic skills—which may not be much compensation for what they lose.

Emotional

It is often the same male attitudes which contribute to the failure of their marriages which make divorce so much more painful for them when it happens. This may be tied in with issues which go far deeper. Many men, especially those who are lacking maturity, may regard (unconsciously or not) their wives as mothers, or at least nurturers. When the maternal attachment figure abandons, then the world collapses. One man, divorced by his wife for 'unreasonable behaviour', and who subsequently committed suicide, said of her:

Vivienne was my nurse.

Men, traditionally less able to recognize and articulate their emotions, are unlikely to have accrued the sort of support network that women seem better at. The emphasis in male groups tends to be more on shared activity than feelings, and drinking or football, squash or business trips will not provide many opportunities to ventilate emotion. Despite the recent rash of male (non-porno) publications on the newsagents' shelves, there is still scarcely the same wealth of 'advice' and information on the subject that flows from the plethora of women's magazines. If they have difficulty revealing their true feelings to their mates or colleagues, then they will emphasize the positive side of their 'freedom', and bury the pain.

A *Daily Express* survey in 1984 revealed that far from revelling in new-found freedom, more than 50 per cent of divorced men interviewed wanted a reconciliation with their wives, and even one in four of the men who started divorce proceedings themselves wished to get back together with their former partners:

> I'm not ashamed to admit I've cried over it. I know I'm to blame, that I didn't recognize what I had until I lost it. If Anne would give me another chance I would do anything. At the office I let them think I'm having a hell of a good time... all the married guys think, 'Lucky sod', but if only they knew the truth... [5]

Significant emotions are anger and bitterness, which in proportion to the other negative effects experienced after divorce, could be long-lasting:

> One might expect that things would get better with time, but matters are not that simple. [Those] who said the effects had been disastrous and permanent had been divorced, on average, more than four years ago and were still feeling that way.[6]

Denial

Men have a greater capacity for denial than women, and may therefore often stick at this stage in coming to terms with the loss of their marriage and its concomitant pain and distress. Tom Leary, a marital therapist and Anglican priest, said:

> *Men especially [want to remarry, and if they want a church wedding they go off to the vicar and] say, 'I was too young. It didn't mean anything.' They have written off the failure of their relationship, or they blame their partner. Women work things through more.*

The marriage and partnership research charity, One plus

One[7], says that because men are less likely to be the instigators of the divorce process, they are more likely to try and deny the reality of marital breakdown, which the authors call:

> a maladaptive coping mechanism associated with a greater chance of ill-health.

Attitudes to women

Another study[8] noted a marked ambivalence on the part of divorced men to women:

> ... It appears that the average divorced man has to reconcile some rather mixed feelings as he seeks out new friends of the opposite sex; he is somewhat more rapacious, somewhat less confident and extremely mistrustful.

Of these, the authors found that mistrust of women was the most profound. Divorced men are particularly vulnerable within new intimate relationships.

Health

The strain of marital breakdown and its side-effects, and the strong emotions associated with it, take an immense toll on men's health. What we do not speak out, we act out, and both our bodies and minds will bear the brunt of what has happened to us. Men are especially vulnerable if they are unable to be in touch with their emotions and express them.

Leonard

Leonard and Sheila had been married twenty-five years. When Sheila left Leonard and the family split—the two sons siding with their mother, and the daughter with their father—Leonard coped during the divorce process but then became ill as he contemplated the emotional, social and financial destruction of the life he had known, and was sacked from his firm. It was only after two years, and through nursing his daughter after a car accident, that Leonard really came back to life again.

Evidence from a considerable body of research[9] shows that the risk of premature death and a wide range of illnesses, including cancer and heart disease, for divorced men is greater than that for divorced women. Mental hospital admissions are higher for divorced men than women, and increased alcohol consumption (with its attendant risks of accident) is a typically masculine response to marital breakdown. Divorced or separated men have also the highest rate of 'unsafe' sex, thereby increasing the risk of HIV-related diseases. Many symptoms which newly-single men have are consistent with anxiety or depression: headaches, listlessness, panic attacks, weight loss (or gain), bowel and stomach disorders and chest pain. Whereas women are more prone to depression generally, men are more likely to commit suicide.

These gender differences, which are consistent, may be explained by the fact that men thrive particularly in marriage, which may also be conducive to a healthier lifestyle since wives often influence their husbands' eating, smoking and drinking habits.

We said in the previous chapter that those who initiate divorce, and who are thus more in control of the process and of their emotions, fare better than the 'passive' partner. Since it is women who (in England and Wales) instigate around 75 per cent of divorces, then this 'desertion' will severely damage self-esteem and be an affront to their partner's masculinity—for stereotypically it is the male who is seen as the one who does the 'roaming'. Women (especially those who work) also tend to remain in the marital home, and thus do not often have the added stress of moving house or area, and gain more support from their surrounding environment.

Social and professional

One of the unhappy paradoxes of men post-divorce is that those who do not gain custody of their children suffer acutely from this (which often goes hand in hand with the loss of home) but those men who do have the care of their children are affected noticeably in the areas of finance and career. Nevertheless, custodial fathers tended to be more positive:

> ... over half of them express positive changes in how they see themselves and, despite the extra work involved in bringing up children, describe positive changes in their relationships with them. Moreover most of them still maintain their original family and friendship network.[10]

A sad sight is to see fast-food restaurants at the weekend crowded with fathers taking out the children they infrequently see, and in such a strange and stilted way. It is not infrequent for non-custodial fathers to move away and lose touch with their children within five years of divorce. This relocation also causes them to maintain fewer and weaker support networks, and adversely affects career chances. Custodial parents, including fathers, often have to sacrifice their careers for their children.

All these factors can add up to drastic life changes, with all the attendant stress and anguish that they produce. Researchers[11] have noted that the negative effects of divorce on men are often interlinked. Those who suffer particularly in one of the areas detailed above were also likely to feel acutely the effects of several others.

'Her' divorce

In general, women cope better with divorce, but saying that in no way denies the pain of the event and its aftermath.

Why women cope better

Two of the main clues to coping post-divorce are: the network of support surrounding the divorcee (women tend to make and maintain these far better than men), and the ability to be in touch with their feelings and verbalize them. Because of these, women manage loss better and may be less isolated emotionally. If women have custody of their children, then their caring and home-making skills will still be required, and this brings with it some sense of worth and value—another significant clue to coping. Even at the turn of the twentieth/twenty-first century there are traditional attitudes which can turn to a woman's advantage: families and friends will tend to be more angry with the husband, expecting that he should do his 'duty' by his wife and children, and so a woman often has the impression that there are still people 'on her side', and gain support and encouragement from that. Jack Dominian says:

> Women are more able to look after themselves and fashion homes, and they cope with isolation better. This still applies, even now. Marriages start off egalitarian but often revert to traditional roles when children come along, and this helps a woman if the couple split up.

Emotional reactions

When husbands walk out it is often well on into the marriage, and women feel the stigma of this keenly. Words such as: shame, disgrace, humiliation and failure recurred regularly in interviews with deserted wives. Women who sue for divorce usually do so earlier in the marriage than men. This may be accounted for by their realization that either marriage or their spouse does not match up to the expectations they had pre-marriage.

What emerged from interviews from divorced women, and from studies of female divorcees, is that there is a significant distinction in recovery from the pain and negativity induced by divorce between younger (pre-menopausal) women, who fare better, and those who had been married for over twenty years and whose children had in general left home.

Gina and Sayeed
Gina left Sayeed (who was of Pakistani origin) after two years of marriage, during which time they had no children. They had married, against Gina's parents' wishes, without fully exploring their expectations of each other. Less than a year into the marriage Gina was saying, 'This man is not the husband I thought he was going to be.' Sayeed, under the pressures of building up his own small business, was unable to hear what she was saying, and one day Gina suddenly left. She knew she could not have stayed but was unsure of what she'd lost.

Jane
Jane was forty-five when her husband left her and went to live with an old girlfriend. In an attempt to repress the pain Jane did what she considered to be all the 'right' things very quickly: she moved area, bought new clothes, made herself a new image, went to aerobics classes. Because she tried to deny reality, she did nothing to resolve her feelings about what had happened and also succeeded in cutting herself off from other people. Jane 'went under', and was on medication for more than a year till she was able to cope again.

Negativity

Although better copers, women often hang on to their negative feelings after divorce for longer than men. Judith Wallerstein[12] says that for nearly half the women in her ten-year study feelings of anger, sexual jealousy, guilt, nostalgia and longing were active forces in their lives. Anger and bitterness at having been exploited and rejected were high in their agenda, and feelings of hurt and humiliation were still intensely painful. In some cases these emotions towards their former husbands were mingled with contempt and pity.

Wallerstein also confirms that it is in general those women who have been married longest at the time of divorce who suffer most and more enduringly:

> It may be that the most realistic expectation in outcome following divorce, especially for women who have been married for a significant portion of their adult lives, is the persistence of powerful, angry feelings and that the most attainable goal is in the encapsulation of these feelings rather than their resolution.[13]

In other words, a complete working through of the pain may not be possible, but what is possible is to learn to live with it peaceably, accepting it, and perhaps allowing it to be transformed into energy.

In Wallerstein's study none of the women who had been in their forties or older at divorce had remarried, nor had formed subsequent stable love relationships. In contrast, all of their former husbands had remarried, except one who was living with a homosexual lover. Anxiety at living alone was far greater among these women, and one woman threatened to commit suicide when her last child left home. Stress levels and depression were higher among older divorcees, and with them the usual crop of psychosomatic symptoms, which themselves made life less bearable for the sufferers.

The research interviews done for this book bore this out completely.

It is a striking paradox that women, especially in the older age range, are proud of what they have done on their own, and at having achieved a great deal they would never have thought possible. Yet the resulting increase in self-esteem and sense of worth, and in what Wallerstein calls 'psychological functioning' during their divorced years (64 per cent of the women in her study showed an improvement) do not go hand in hand with any lessening of the animosity they feel towards their former spouses. They see themselves as failures, however much they had achieved professionally and socially, for they had failed in their goal of remaining happily married, and for that they are bitter and resentful.

Another paradox and a factor which may be linked with this continuing bitterness and lack of forgiveness is that women, generally more self-aware and emotionally literate than men, are reluctant to shoulder responsibility for marital breakdown, whereas men—if not stuck in denial—are more willing to admit liability for the failure (once they have accepted the breakdown). According to Wallerstein, women tended to blame causes outside themselves, such as their husband's infidelity, bad moods, absence from home, or lack of financial support.

Loneliness

Loneliness is one of the greatest problems for the divorcing or divorced woman, and—in a third paradox—it seems that this feeling of loneliness is not always mitigated by stronger support groups of friends, family and sometimes colleagues:

I have so many needs too. I want to be truly loved for me, not sex, just plain old love. I want to be looked after for once in my life, really looked after and really cared for. Will it ever happen or is God the only one who loves me as I am?

Economic plight

Women whose marriages have followed the traditional model of husband=breadwinner, wife=homemaker (and that is more usually the case in the upper age range or in some cases where there are young children), will be more dependent on their husbands financially, and less able to support themselves when their marriages end. If the divorce settlement is inequitable, or if there is simply not enough cake to be sliced up for the man's former and current households, or he will not pay, then the plight of economically-dependent women can be hard indeed, forcing them to rely on state hand-outs and, in some cases where it is possible, family. This only adds to feelings of humiliation and degradation:

> *It's been five years now. He just never turns up in court, and we don't get a penny. There's always some excuse. How can he get away with it? Don't we count for anything?*

Social identity

Again, it was older divorced women whose social identity was bound up more in their married role and status, and to some extent in his professional status and their standard of living. When this ended the image of self was smashed, and had to be gradually built up anew in a different context. To them this was failure; they had invested their whole selves in something which now did not exist, and they too often felt annihilated.

> *I'm simply now*
> *An unwanted wife.*
> TANYA PALMER

Nevertheless, apart from the older divorcees, whose post-divorce suffering was palpable in the interviews, women managed to create lives for themselves which were not devoid of meaning and pleasure. Those who worked through the causes of failure of their first marriages and came to terms with the negativity it left them with were more likely to have happier subsequent partnerships, though in some cases the same patterns were seen to repeat up to two or three more times. Wallerstein's study found, too, that over a period of years women rather than men seemed to enhance their quality of life after divorce, in terms of the nature and quality of interpersonal relationships, general contentment, freedom from neurotic suffering, and socio-economic status and stability.

Few would have predicted this enhancement in their lives at the time of separation, when suffering huge emotional strain and anxiety:

> Perhaps more unexpected was a new and disarming directness in acknowledging needs and expressing thoughts and feelings, as well as a newfound capacity to employ humour. Most of all, we noted an outlook which was keenly realistic and unsentimental in its appraisal of self and the world, which contrasted sharply with our earlier observations of these same women at the time of the original separation.[14]

Pain, if we allow ourselves to feel it and live it and learn from it, is far more a springboard to growth than are ease and complacency.

1. Christopher Clulow (Tavistock Institute of Marital Studies) St Catharine's Conference Report no 30, 'Marriage: Trends and Implications'.

2. Penny Mansfield and Jean Collard, *The Beginning of the Rest of Your Life? A Portrait of newly-wed Marriage*, Macmillan, 1988, page 39.

3. H.D. Skuse et al, reported in *Nature* no. 387, 1997 pages 703—708.

4. Judith M. Wallerstein, *Women after Divorce: Preliminary report from a Ten-Year Follow-Up*, American Journal of Orthopsychiatry, 56 [1], January 1986.

5. Quoted in 'How do men feel about divorce?', *Woman's World*, September 1984.

6. Peter Ambrose, John Harper, Richard Pemberton, *Surviving Divorce, Men beyond Marriage*, Wheatsheaf Books, 1983 page 111.

7. *Marital Breakdown and the Health of the Nation*, ed. Fiona McAllister, One plus One, 1995 (second edition), page 10.
8. Peter Ambrose *(see note 6)*, page 132ff.
9. *Marital Breakdown and the Health of the Nation (see note 7)*.
10. *Marital Breakdown and the Health of the Nation (see note 7)*, page 110.
11. *Marital Breakdown and the Health of the Nation (see note 7)*, page 125.
12. Judith M. Wallerstein, *(see note 4)*.
13. Judith M. Wallerstein, *(see note 4)*.
14. Judith M. Wallerstein, *(see note 4)*.

10

Religion—consolation or condemnation?

> The rules are anachronistic. They were made when divorce
> wasn't common. That's not the case now. All the church is
> doing by refusing to countenance divorce is making a lot
> of people unhappy... [1]

The age in which we live has been called 'post-Christian'. The
secularization of society means that relatively few people today
are acquainted with either the ethos or the strictures of living a
Christian faith. However, many people still desire to be married
in church, and are aware that there is some sort of spiritual
dimension to their marriage. When divorcees wish to be
married in church they will often find that there is an obstacle,
and this can cause hurt and anger.

This chapter examines briefly the stance on divorce and
remarriage of the major Christian denominations in the United
Kingdom, and looks also at the Jewish and Muslim positions. It
draws on the testimony of some who have suffered from what
could be seen as a legalistic lack of charity on the part of the
churches concerned, and urges some compassionate pastoral
solutions for divorced Christians.

For those who are committed to their Christian faith, the
question of divorce and remarriage can add immensely to the
agony of breaking up. Not only may they believe that divorce is
contrary to the will of God, but conscience—or their pastors—
may prevent them contracting a second union in the belief that

marriage is life-long and indissoluble. This renders any relationship (even following a civil ceremony) adulterous. Some may feel—and be—ostracized by their fellow worshippers, and Roman Catholics are likely to be refused the sacrament of Holy Communion if they are in what the Catholic Church calls 'an irregular situation':

> The church, like society, has been overwhelmed by divorce because it does not understand the change in marriage, and so throws law at people as a way of defending the institution. This doesn't work. The church is often a poor mother to those whose marriages have broken down—she does not always nurture, and can and does add to the pain and trauma.
>
> JACK DOMINIAN

Yet, whatever our religious belief, divorce may be the only option open to us for many reasons. Our partner may demand it, may desert the home, and in certain relationships there may exist such a relational 'terrorism'—a sort of endemic violence—that one or other partner may feel obliged to flee from a relationship which is destructive and devouring, whatever the spiritual price to be paid.

Christian marriage

> The church gave us no support on the sacramental side of our marriage. This is the church's role—to explore 'for better, for worse' at the sharp end. The church should help people to develop as people within the sacrament of marriage—but it's lacking.
>
> MALE DIVORCEE, 55

The Christian understanding of marriage is based on, firstly, the book of Genesis, in which God creates a companion for Adam.

The account tells us 'That is why a man leaves his father and mother and is united to his wife, and the two become one flesh' (Genesis chapter 2, verse 24)[2]. In the Gospels Jesus refers back to this and says 'What therefore God has joined together, let not man put asunder.' But it is not just that Jesus sets an ideal for male-female relationships to which couples should aspire; in both Old and New Testaments the union of husband and wife is symbolic of God's covenant with His people, an alliance which cannot be broken:

> I will betroth you to myself for ever, betroth you in lawful wedlock with unfailing devotion and love; I will betroth you to myself to have and to hold, and you shall know the Lord. (Hosea, chapter 2 verses 19–20)

> Husbands, love your wives, as Christ also loved the church and gave himself up for it. (Paul's letter to the Ephesians, chapter 5 verse 25)

In this way Christian marriage is seen as being imbued with a mystical significance: the union of man and woman in matrimony mirrors the intimacy of our personal relationship with our Creator, made possible by Jesus' self-giving love.

This high ideal masks an underlying and deep-rooted malaise on the part of the institutional church at anything which concerns the expression of sexuality, and it seems that this can be countenanced only when safely contained within marriage. For many Christians any trespass over these safe boundaries appears to engender a sexual insecurity which translates itself in judgmentalism.[3]

The Church of England

'Bishop and divorcee to marry at register office'—said the newspaper headlines in the spring of 1997, when the Bishop of Birmingham, Mark Santer, announced his intention to marry a long-divorced friend of his late wife's. In 1994 the Rev. Kit Chalcraft, twice divorced, was relieved of his living by the Bishop of Norwich because his averred desire to marry a third time did not 'bear witness effectively to Christian standards of marriage'. The current heir to the throne of the United Kingdom, who will become Supreme Governor of the Church of England, was himself divorced and admitted to a long-standing adulterous liaison.

The Church of England believes marriage is for life, and yet it is obvious from the behaviour of its bishops and clergy that it has moved a long way from the inflexibility of this high ideal, which caused the young Princess Margaret to renounce Group Captain Peter Townsend, a divorced man, because she was 'mindful of the teaching of the church'. Indeed, since 1991 divorced and remarried candidates for ordination have been selected, and it is not usually seen as a bar to being in charge of a parish.

The debate on divorce at General Synod in December 1994 typifies the lack of cohesion in the Anglican position, which caused the then Archbishop of York, Dr John Habgood, to proclaim that

> One of the disgraces as the world sees it is that the church has been so far unable to come to any co-ordinated policy.

This was echoed by the Ven. George Austen, Archdeacon of York:

> The C of E is beginning to be held in contempt by many people because we are ready to throw aside our principles.

Many spoke up against the remarriage of divorcees in church, saying a willingness on the church's part to marry someone who may have deserted a wife or husband and children was in effect saying to the abandoned partner that the church condoned the breakup of the family. However, the Bishop of Sodor and Man's appeal for the Synod to 'give a firm message that we uphold the sanctity of marriage and that we refuse to be led by the nose by sentimental hype' seems at variance with what is increasingly common practice, for it is not difficult to find an Anglican parson who will marry divorcees, though these must of course fulfil a residence requirement within his parish. It is left to the discretion of the priest, who must inform the local bishop.

However, such things can divide parishes:

> We knew that the PCC wouldn't want us to marry in church. It was all rather silly. We both play a full part in the life of the church. They accepted us as single people, when we were divorcees, and accepted us once we were a married couple—they just wouldn't let us get married… It's not a case of changing morals, it's a question of changing facts… At the moment it's confused where it should be clear-cut, causing division and argument. The CoE's reputation is becoming one of a church that can't make up its mind.[4]

Locally, inflexible beliefs can lead to painful pastoral situations. One deacon, since ordained priest, refused not only to take part in but even to attend his divorced sister's second wedding, and in one case a group of charismatic Anglicans, some of whom were elders of their parish church, boycotted the wedding of their PCC secretary to a divorced man.

But the net result of the Church of England's fudging accommodations is a generally compassionate face to those who regret the failure of their first marriage, and who wish to witness publicly to the love in their new relationship by marrying. Certainly, there is no question of deprivation of communion for those in second marriages. However, a 'Surviving Divorce' group from Shropshire wrote a plea to the Church of England which hints at the pain at being divorced and a practising Anglican:

> Please acknowledge that the separation or divorce has happened, and does happen to people in congregations. Please don't ignore us even if you don't know what to say. Most of us felt very much alone... Some of us would still want to be asked to do things in the church.[5]

The Methodist Church

The Methodist Church has recently reviewed its position on 'the marriage of divorced persons', which was formerly encapsulated in a statement made in 1946[6], in response to 'the many changes in society and church thinking about marriage and divorce.' Their broad and flexible viewpoint is that when a married couple divorce, their marriage is 'completely and absolutely' at an end, and that is why they speak of the 'marriage' of divorced persons and not 'remarriage'.

Methodists acknowledge that

> ... in appropriate circumstances marriage after divorce may be an honourable, healing and enriching experience, and blessed by God.[7]

However, they do accept that some of their members may believe that a second marriage (where the previous partner still lives) is always contrary to the will of God. If an individual minister cannot in conscience conduct such a wedding, then the couple must nevertheless be pointed in the direction of a minister who has no conscientious objections.

The Methodist Church, in its public declarations on the subject, demonstrates a pastoral sensitivity to the people involved in divorce and subsequent marriage, and urges especial pastoral care to be devoted to:

■ the encouragement of the growth of true friendship between the divorced couple—while not ignoring the effect this may have on any new relationship;

■ the well-being of the children;

■ support of any adults involved in the welfare of the children;

■ the emotional, psychological and spiritual health of divorced people.

On the last point the Methodist Church recognizes the crippling feelings of guilt and failure inherent in the breakdown and termination of a marriage, and the breaching of the marriage vows ('for better for worse… till death us do part') and is exploring the possibility of a liturgy for release from vows.

The United Reformed Church

The stance of the United Reformed Church is in essence similar to that of the Methodists in that its emphasis is bringing God's love and healing into the pastoral situation.

When a marriage is in trouble the URC seeks first to bring about reconciliation, because it believes that Christian marriage is ideally a lifelong relationship that can overcome difficulties. If this cannot be, the URC seeks to minister to those suffering 'the deep sense of failure and… loneliness'[8] which results. The URC document, however, notes that this does not always happen 'on the ground':

Church members sometimes add to these burdens by lack of understanding and concern... the church also needs to show compassion for those who fail to maintain the ideal in a marriage relationship but who still hold a Christian view of marriage.

The conditions for marrying again within the URC are:

■ that a state divorce has already taken place;

■ that the issues surrounding the breakup of the former marriage have been discussed with the minister, and any problems (for example, concerning the care of children) have been satisfactorily resolved.

In some cases where a divorcee wishes to remarry (and here the URC emulates the Orthodox Churches, and is ahead of Methodists and Anglicans) it is possible to hold a service of 'Prayer for Release from Vows', in which penitence is expressed for the failure of the previous marriage, and recognition that it is now ended and a desire to seek a new beginning are made explicit.

The Baptist Union of Great Britain

The Baptist Church in Great Britain is a union of independent local congregations, which means that there is no hierarchical government to decide policy on behalf of the churches. Thus decisions on the marriage of divorced persons in the Baptist Church reside with the chapel concerned. These can and do differ, with some adopting the compassionate pastoral approach of the Methodists and URC, but others (and the Grace [Strict] Baptists are a case in point) sometimes—and no doubt unwittingly—adding to the sense of failure, guilt and spiritual and personal inadequacy that someone whose marriage has broken down may feel. But inflexibility, wherever it is made to be felt, can and does result in 'pressure cooker' situations where further damage is done because true feelings cannot be expressed or received with honesty. In strict Baptist circles couples have remained 'together' where there has been prolonged adultery, or even cruelty, because of the grip the chapel has on their lives.

The Roman Catholic Church

I am thinking in particular of thousands of Catholics who are living in a truly loving second marriage and yet are barred, at least officially, from taking Communion... These are the sort of community problems, awkward and difficult as they may be, which need to be recognized and tackled if we are going to avoid the risk of allowing our practice to contradict our message.One parishioner, whom I know to be an excellent mother and caring wife, persevered in coming to Mass for over twenty-five years before she felt able to take Communion again. Her husband had been previously married. Today she feels certain that her five grown-up children would still be practising Catholics had she been allowed to participate more fully in the Mass and the community life of her parish. Her children, she told me, found it difficult to understand why she should continue when the Church barred her from Holy Communion and considered her to be living in sin.[9]

Roman Catholic divorcees who wish to remarry are the most likely to find encounters with their church bruising and painful, as this parish priest writes above.

In the Roman Catholic Church, marriage is held to be a sign of God's love (that is, a sacrament), which means spouses carry a heavy burden of responsibility. Roman Catholic spouses are enjoined to express the ideal of human heterosexual love which reflects God's love for His people, no less. It is irrevocable and it is total:

> The married couple forms the intimate partnership of life and love established by the Creator and governed by his laws; it is rooted in the conjugal covenant, that is, in their irrevocable personal consent. Both give themselves definitively and totally to one another. They are no longer two; from now on they form one flesh. The covenant they freely contracted imposes on the spouses the obligation to preserve it as unique and indissoluble... Fidelity expresses constancy in keeping one's given word. God is faithful. The sacrament of matrimony enables man and woman to enter into Christ's fidelity for His Church... they bear witness to this mystery before the world.[10]

Roman Catholics who practise their faith and who are divorced may suffer in profound and long-lasting ways because of the intransigence of the official teaching on divorce and remarriage, and it may seem to them that they are being victimized for failing to live up to the expectation loaded upon them by a church which cannot recognize the wrong of living with someone when the relationship is dead.

Further, the Roman Catholic Church states that

> The remarriage of persons divorced from a living, lawful spouse contravenes the plan and law of God as taught by Christ. They are not separated from the Church, but they cannot receive eucharistic communion.[11]

and adds, as though there were no doubt about the matter:

> They will lead Christian lives especially by educating their children in the faith.

The Roman Catholic Church will, under certain conditions, decree that a marriage of people who have gone through a civil divorce is nul (more commonly called 'granting an annulment'), which is a decision made by a diocesan tribunal after much investigation of whether the marriage was valid in the first place. For canon lawyers and theologians marriage is still viewed as a contract, and if a contract is not correctly drawn up and witnessed it becomes nul. It must be entered into freely by people who both know what they are doing and are able to fulfil what they undertake.

And how many of us can say that about our nuptials?

Annulment is not dissolution of a marriage by the back door. Canon lawyers will argue that the conditions needed for a life-long commitment were never present in the marriages they annul.

But it can take a lot of heart-rending and soul-searching to go through the investigations of the tribunal; it may also depend on the unforthcoming cooperation of the former spouse and in-laws and friends, and—though the Roman Catholic Church claims it is a cathartic and thus a healing process—it often opens old wounds. So what of those who do not or cannot go through it? What of those who go through it but whose marriages are not declared nul? What of those, remarried, waiting years for a decision? These people are deemed to be in 'irregular situations' and unless they can find a diocese with a lenient bishop, or a compassionate priest, more interested in the love of Christ than a strict adherence to the rules or the avoidance of 'scandal', they will be denied the eucharist. It is the same people who, broken and wounded by failure, need the comfort of the sacrament.

There is scope at parish level for sensitive and compassionate solutions, which need not lack integrity. The Roman Catholic Church has always preached the supremacy of personal conscience (the 'internal forum'—one's responsibility before God, rather than to the church), and enlightened pastors are increasingly bringing to bear the notion of *epikaeia*, which is the temporary suspension of the law in favour of justice where the enforcement of a rule brings about an injustice; in other words, the application of the *principle* behind the rule, rather than the rule itself. God's grace, his love and forgiveness come free; the question for the church should always be, 'What would Jesus have done?'

The Orthodox Churches

The Western Church, and in particular the Roman Catholic Church, could—in a spirit of ecumenism—learn much from the spirituality and practice of the mainstream Orthodox Churches.

Firstly, the Eastern Churches have been imaginative in both preparation and forms of worship by instructing couples in a commitment to indissoluble fidelity in marriage, and— secondly—by teaching on healing forgiveness, making every effort to mend and heal those relationships which are capable of it.

On the question of divorce, the Orthodox Churches regard the moral death of a marriage (the painful collapse, or destruction, of a marriage intended to be permanent) as something perhaps even more serious and radical than the physical death of a spouse. It happens not because of any one-off act of infidelity or cruelty, but when living together actually seems to be working against the salvation and integrity of either partner. There can be no question of a rapid entry into another marriage, and a period of mourning is required not just to heal the pain of separation, but also the deep wounds which have occurred during the union. The Catholic theologian Bernard Häring[12] writes:

Someone who has just lost a spouse through the moral

death of a marriage needs our profoundest sympathy.

Within the worldwide Orthodox Church the blessing of a second marriage, once the due period of mourning and coming to terms with the reason for the death of the first marriage are completed, is permitted. Although the various churches have different forms of ritual for this, there is one thing common to all of them: the failure of the first marriage is solemnly brought to mind; God's patience and mercy are emphasized; healing and peace are prayed for. The second marriage is always seen and celebrated within the embrace of the healing and merciful love of God, the 'divine father of the household' (*oicónomoz*). A third marriage is generally not granted.

Judaism

> Divorce is still the sort of thing which 'does not happen' in a good Jewish family, which is one of the reasons why these families need a lot of help.[13]

For Orthodox Jews divorce is admitted in law. If divorce is by mutual consent then the Jewish law of *Halacha* provides a clean and swift way out of marriage—no need for bitterness or proof of grounds. In Reform and Liberal Jewish communities husband and wife have complete equality, and a one-sided divorce has to have a reason. But among Orthodox Jews the woman can still get a raw deal. Orthodox Jewish couples who wish to divorce must go through the procedure for civil divorce, and have to appear before a *Beth Din*, a religious court, and apply for divorce.

The unfairness lies in the fact that it is the man who gives the '*Get*'—the deed of divorce which is handed to the former spouse. The wife must either receive it, or refuse it. But in the latter case it makes no difference—the husband is free to walk away and start a new life with another (but unmarried) woman. Any children of that union will be kosher. But a woman who is denied a *Get* out of her husband's vindictiveness is stuck for life. She cannot remarry, and any children she may have from a subsequent relationship (even if she remarries in a Reform or Liberal synagogue) are deemed illegitimate and *mamzerim* (denied their place as children of Israel).

There are other problems for Orthodox Jews. The *agunah* (the abandoned wife or 'woman in chains'), whose husband is disqualified in law from giving a *Get* because of insanity, or who merely walks out on her, has little recourse to justice. In theory, rabbis can grant an annulment to a woman who can prove that the marriage was a terrible mistake from the first and they can ostracize a man who refuses his wife a *Get* (he can be barred from the synagogue and cold-shouldered in his business) but in practice it seems that Orthodox rabbis often take the side of the man.

But things are changing for Jewish couples. Reforms in Canada and the United States brought about by the International Coalition for Agunah Rights (ICAR), are influencing practice among Jews in Great Britain. Mandatory pre-nuptial contracts in the United Synagogue will make it impossible for a man to refuse his wife a *Get* once the civil divorce has been granted.

The number of divorces is rising in the Jewish community as it is elsewhere, but divorcees, especially women, can find their *shul* (synagogue community) cool and unhelpful. Two young Jewish women divorcees spoke to the *Jewish Chronicle* of their difficulties:

I wanted to start a small support group for single parents so I contacted my synagogue. The secretary was unhelpful. She told me: 'There are loads of activities here and we have no spare rooms. You can only meet if you have a large group.'

'I joined another *shul*—so I wouldn't embarrass them at social gatherings.' [14]

Islam

According to Muslim understanding, the law (or *Shari'ah*) confers equal dignity on both men and women, who have the same religious duties, and in some case the same legal rights. But gender differentiations (believed to be divinely revealed in the *Qur'an*) make for a quite different practice, when it comes to marriage and divorce.

Muslims believe it is a human duty to marry, because procreation is the divine aim. The ideal family structure is based on monogamy, which has been the normal practice among Muslims in the UK, although the *Shari'ah* allows polygamy under certain circumstances.

The whole area of divorce is complex, but in essence the position is that it is easier and simpler for a man to divorce his wife than vice versa. At the time of marriage, and included in the marriage contract, the man specifies a sum of money which he will pay to his spouse in settlement in the event of his subsequently repudiating her. If a man wishes to divorce his wife he has only to call two witnesses at three times over a three month period, hand over the cash payment, and the marriage is at an end. A Muslim woman does not have the right to divorce her husband. If she wishes to end her marriage she has to go to the Muslim Council, who will consider her case. The grounds for divorce are generally that the wife cannot bear children, which is still seen as the vital part of the marriage. Wanting to marry another woman, because it is so often permitted, is not an issue for divorce.

A Muslim woman divorced, therefore, especially for 'infertility', may have a hard time in her community, which may show intolerance, lack of provision and ostracism.[15]

Arranged marriages

Many Muslim marriages, and those of other Eastern religions are arranged, usually by parents. The general feeling is that these are often successful in so far as couples stay together, but expectations are not so high, and there is a lack of emphasis on personal fulfilment in relationship, and divorce has been more difficult. A Muslim wife, Shabnam Zia, a graduate, who is in an arranged marriage to a chemical engineer in Karachi said:

> In an arranged marriage, you expect nothing and you are mentally poised to adjust to life with a stranger. In love marriages you enter with the highest expectations, and if they are not fulfilled, the relationship shatters.[16]

But things are changing, and westernization is having its effect. A decade or so ago divorce was a rarity, mainly because women had such lowly status and few rights. In 1997 New Delhi's four matrimonial courts were processing 100,000 petitions for divorce. In March of that year the parents of a Pakistani woman sought to have her love match annulled. The court refused.

Where traditional religion loses its grip, divorce statistics rise.

People who are going through, or who are recovering from, divorce are wounded; it is not only the marriage which is broken, often it is their hearts, their spirits, their lives as well. If they belong to a Christian or Jewish group—church, chapel or synagogue—it is a chance for the members of that community to live the faith they proclaim, and act in cooperation with the God in whose image we believe we are made, whether this is the God of the Old Testament:

> It is he who heals the broken in spirit
> and binds up their wounds[17]

...What is it that the Lord asks of you?
Only to act justly, to love loyalty...[18]

or of the New:

Pass no judgment, and you will not be judged. For as you
judge others, so you will yourselves be judged...[19]

He comforts us in all our troubles, so that we in turn may be
able to comfort others in any trouble of theirs and to share
with them the consolation we ourselves receive from God. [20]

Those who believe in Jesus Christ will know that just as love
can be costly and painful, so also can pain be healed by self-
giving love—in the words of the old hymn:

'Love to the loveless shown, that they may lovely be.'[21]

This is the mission of the church to those broken on the rack
of failed relationship. The ideal is expressed by a divorced
Roman Catholic woman:

Seven years ago I had personal experience of this kind of
loving support when my marriage of almost thirty years
broke down and the bottom seemed to fall out of my
world. I was surrounded by love, understanding and
acceptance and cherished within the community until I
could rebuild my self-esteem and rethink my role in life—
my vocation from God—and was never allowed to feel that
my situation in any way altered my place within the
community. [22]

1. From *The Independent*, 3 December, 1994.
2. Biblical quotations are from the New English Bible
3. For a fuller discussion of sex and gender issues in the church, see Mary Kirk and Tom Leary,

Holy Matrimony?, Lynx Communications, 1994.

4. From *The Independent*, 3 December, 1994.

5. *Something to Celebrate, Valuing Families in Church and Society*, Report of a Working Party of the Board of Social Responsibility, © The Central Board of Finance of the Church of England, Church House Publishing, 1995, page 176.

6. Standing Order 830 of the Methodist Conference.

7. *Marriage of Divorced Persons*, Report to Conference 1994, The Methodist Church Division of Social Responsibility.

8. *Remarriage—URC Practice*, document issued by the United Reformed Church.

9. 'The language of love' by ' Pastor Ignotus', in 'Parish Diary', *The Tablet*, 31 May, 1997.

10. *Catechism of the Catholic Church*, 1994 Latin text copyright Libreria Editrice Vaticana, Città del Vaticano; English translation for the UK 1994 Geoffrey Chapman.

11. *As note 10.*

12. *No Way Out? Pastoral Care of the Divorced and Remarried*, Bernard Häring, St Paul Publications, 1989.

13. Ellenruth Susskind, then chair of the Anglo-Jewish Divorce and Conciliation Project, quoted in the *Jewish Chronicle*, 16 March, 1984.

14. *Jewish Chronicle*, 1 October, 1982.

15. Information from *Religions in the UK—a multi-faith directory*, 1993, and the Asian Family Counselling Service.

16. Quoted in 'Tying the Knots (Making Matches)' by Tony Clifton in *Newsweek*, 9 June, 1997.

17. Psalm 147, verse 3.

18. Micah chapter 6, verse 8.

19. Matthew chapter 7, verses 1-2.

20. 2 Corinthians, chapter 1 verse 4

21. 'My song is love unknown', Samuel Crossman c 1624-83.

22. Anne Smith, 'Working together for the glory of God', in *Priests and People*, volume 11 number 6, June 1997.

PART 3

Life after divorce

11

Shadows from the past

What we shall be in the future is influenced by the past, and our future contains within it elements of both past and present.

There are whole shelves of books devoted to the lifetime task of emerging from the grieving process of divorce. For the most part their cautiously optimistic titles—variations on the themes of 'surviving', 'beginning again', 'loving again', 'trusting', 'becoming'— seek to engender positive thoughts and feelings of hope, though always with the rider that 'much work must be done on yourself before you enter another relationship'.

It is undeniably true that the chaos will subside, that pain will lessen, that we shall grow stronger, become more independent, that from the experience we can learn much of who and what we are and what drives us to act as we do. Happiness and fulfilment *can* be created, and a future relationship *can* succeed.

So why then did the research for this book unearth so much raw human agony, sometimes many years after the event? Why was divorce called a 'life sentence'? Why was the pain unending and crippling? And yet almost invariably those who were crushed by it had had months or years of counselling and therapy, had often had medication to help them, had friends and family to support them. One reason of course is that it was those who, despite professional help, had not yet resolved some of the issues present in their marital breakdown who had the stories to tell, and in telling them sought both relief and perhaps resolution. Another is that it was those who were left rather than those who did the leaving who had the most to say. The fact remains, many 'arrest' in grief, with a greater or lesser degree of handicap in their lives, for many years, if not the rest of their days. Even most of those who had gone on to subsequent marriages—with more or less satisfaction—felt some essential part of themselves had been tarnished by failure or guilt, or both. Often many wished—*even if they had been the leavers*—that it were possible to put the clock back.[1]

The final part of this book looks at whether it is possible to live again fully and happily after divorce, and how this can be achieved. It will say that there are no easy answers, and those that there are sound trite to the ears of someone engulfed in misery, loss and a maelstrom of change and emotion. Many of those interviewed seemed to apologise for the fact that they could not yet quite make the most of their single state:

I was divorced sixteen years ago. I certainly remember the agony of it all as vividly as if it were yesterday. Despite repeated efforts and a lot of optimism in the early years (and even now), I'm still trying to repair the damage. I wish I could say something upbeat and encouraging about 'working through' these experiences and coming out the other side, presumably as a 'better, stronger and wiser person', to use all the clichés. Unfortunately I can't, in all honesty.

I was divorced last year, having been separated for six years. I was married for nearly twenty-eight years in what I have always believed to have been a happy and stable union for twenty-seven of those years. Even though I have formed—reasonably successfully—a complete new life for myself, I sometimes feel I shall never get over the hurt my husband has caused both me and my adult children.

It is obvious that any attempt at discovering how to emerge well from divorce must avoid the clichés, and yet it will inevitably sound facile to those still in pain. It must always be remembered, as one divorcee said, that:

It cannot be described unless you have personally experienced it.

179

Negativity

In divorcing we may have been led to doubt our value, our lovableness, our ability to make a relationship work, and these blows to our self esteem will prejudice our chances in future relationships, unless we can somehow use the experience positively. This is surprisingly sometimes true of the leaver as well as of the one who feels rejected or betrayed.

Turning what we see as a failure into something positive is a long haul, and success will be seen only retrospectively, and maybe in surprising ways. Yet we owe it to ourselves, to any future partner, and to those who depend on us, not to commit ourselves to another relationship while we are still awash with the negativity with which divorce has left us. Embarking on an intimate relationship in order to salve the pain of a previous one is unfair to both parties and is unlikely ultimately to succeed either as a relationship or as an anodyne. The shadows from the past will darken our emotional existence, and even if we can never entirely rid ourselves of them, we must render them less harmful by understanding them—and ourselves—better.

'The triumph of hope over experience'

Partnerships which are formed, as more and more are, from halves of a previous couple are doubly fragile. Expectations may run high, whether we are bruised and let down or ebullient and enthusiastic; the will to succeed *this time* will be in inverse ratio to past disappointment and disillusion. Unfortunately, statistics suggest that the 'triumph of hope over experience' leads to a higher rate of relational breakdown, and that it happens sooner in the relationship[2].

Before uniting ourselves with a new lover or spouse we not only have to have grieved the former one but to have left behind the unproductive aspects of the relational system within which we have operated, for if our patterns of relating remain unchanged, so too will the problems they have caused—whoever we are with. It is not the strength of our feelings that keeps us with our partner, but the quality of the relationship each person can offer.

Light on the past

Divorce, if we let it and are honest with ourselves, can shine a torch on what has gone before, on our whole way of relating, on what impelled us in the first place to form, or to take refuge in, an intimate relationship. This searchlight can cast strong and dark shadows on a new relationship, and these will not go away unless we allow the light to penetrate every area of our relational system, which will have been learned young from the way our parents related to each other and to us. If, after years plunged in post-separation grief and depression, we are still unable to mobilize ourselves to live fully, then it suggests that we have never been able to cope with the anguish of separation and lead autonomous lives. To live well as a twosome we first have to be able to live well by ourselves.

One of the darkest shadows on which we must shine the light of truth is that of our needs within an intimate relationship.

The ability to be separate

According to Freudian theory what is called 'separation-individuation' is the task of our early lives, which continues from birth to leaving home and beyond. This is the process by which we learn to become independent beings, capable of existing without being fused with another. Autonomy, although the process of acquiring it goes on throughout childhood and adolescence, has its roots in infancy.

As babies we gradually have to learn to overcome the anguish of 'losing' our mother. In other words, the child must learn to accept being left by its mother without being terrified that she will never return, or experiencing fear of annihilation when she goes away. This developmental stage, the age of nurture (also known as the 'oral' phase), up to around eighteen months, requires 'good enough' maternal care—warmth, food, comfort—all provided reliably. If they are, the child will learn to trust and depend appropriately, cope with frustration reasonably, be able to accept and eventually give care, and have a sense of identity and self-worth.

If we do not get enough of this as small babies (and individual needs may vary from birth) then in adult relationships we may:

- be demanding, clinging and possessive;

- fear abandonment and rejection;

- be capable of violent and destructive anger when we do not get what we want;

- distance any uncomfortable feeling from ourselves, and project it on to others, making the world a hostile place;

- misinterpret others' behaviour;

- expect too much of others;

- be unsure of what we have to offer;

- be totally concerned with ourselves and our own needs;

- develop an addictive personality.

In short, we shall lack self-esteem at a dangerous level. In our relationships we shall not be able to conceptualize love without being 'picked up and held', desiring above all else the complete emotional fusion we once had (but not sufficiently) with our mother. 'Do not leave me' will be our plea, and we may be willing to undergo humiliation and abuse in order to cling on to our partner. 'Separation-individuation', which distinguishes the adult from the emotional child, will not have taken place.

We can become ourselves only in relation to others (neither fused with them nor excluding them). Living in harmony with ourselves means we shall be able to live with others in the complementarity of needs, roles, tasks and functions which is relationship. If we can find the right balance between our desire for freedom (which gives us independence) and our infantile needs (which we all still have to a certain degree, especially in times of pain or stress) for emotional oneness, then we shall be able appropriately to be on our own, with others or in a couple.

But 'appropriately' is a key word here. We must not expect to find in our 'significant other' a nurse or mother; no one will baby us, give us the care we want, pay attention to us *all the time*. We must learn to accept frustration, to believe we are worth something without being mirrored in the admiring eyes of another and to take responsibility for our actions and reactions, and not always blame others. Then we shall be capable of a mature relationship. Those who have not yet acquired autonomy will continually search for someone to shelter them from the slings and arrows of existence. They will be demanding, and others cannot but confirm their deepest terrors by turning and running from such emotional greed.

Similarly, if we are too defensive, cannot let go of ourselves, express our emotions and dare to be vulnerable; if we cannot share our psychological intimacy with someone, we shall not be able to love or be loved truly. We shall be cut off from ourselves and from our profoundest feelings, refusing to admit our need of love or true friendship—because of the anguish at the possibility of being abandoned or betrayed.

Our 'shadow side'

We each of us have a 'shadow' side, the parts we fear will be rejected as unlovely and unlovable if they should be glimpsed by the outside world. These 'shadows' may be areas which our family of origin could not or did not deal with well—for example anger, or sexuality. We learn, often from our youngest days, from the way they habitually dealt with things (the 'family system') that some aspects of ourselves are unacceptable, and we hide these shameful parts of us from view. It is the logic of our unconscious which is trying to protect us from the pain of rejection.

When we fall in love we are, again unconsciously, seeking acceptance and healing for these needy parts of ourselves which we hide or disown. With the eyes of our unconscious we see the shadow side mirrored in our partner, and this thrill of recognition of a 'soul-mate' is often what passes for love. We feel completed and fulfilled. We each become a mirror for the other in which our own personality is reflected back at us; in other words, we project ourselves on to the other. If our partner has similar needs and unhealed wounds they will be able to pick up and decode the unconscious messages we are emitting which are geared to getting what we need. This psychological recognition (added to a reasonable social, intellectual and physical match) often produces a couple who believe they are made for each other:

He was so affectionate, warm and kind. My father was cold and nasty. But my husband's tenderness disappeared when we got married because I was in the bag. The first time he shouted at me was on our honeymoon. I was used to being shouted at because I had a nasty father.

But two sets of unmet needs, of unacknowledged shadowy areas do not necessarily result in the wholeness and healing we are reaching out for. Sometimes our unacceptable characteristics cause us too much pain to 'own', and we defend ourselves by projecting them on to our partner. Often we are unaware of these aspects of our own personalities, and they are the opposite of the ones we admit to.

Nicola and Roger

Nicola had married Roger when she was twenty-one and he was forty. She had been a shy girl, and was attracted to Roger because he seemed mature and caring. They had no children. During the course of their marriage she became increasingly aware that she had to take most of the responsibility not only for their household matters but also for their business—a sub-post office and general stores. Roger was not reliable, given to going off and leaving her in charge without help, and spending too much money. After ten years of marriage, Nicola went to a counsellor, complaining of her husband's irresponsibility. Here she started to understand that even when they had been engaged Roger's immaturity had been apparent, though she had not recognized it then. She also realized that, since her own father had been weak and henpecked by her mother, who had been overbearing and for whom she had little affection, Nicola had looked to Roger for a father's dependable qualities. Although at a conscious level she longed for this sort of support, unconsciously she was determined not to be as submissive and ineffectual as her father had been. In so doing, she had in fact re-enacted her own family's system of relating and became the dominant one, just like her mother. What she had once perceived as Roger's strength and organizational skills were in fact the bossiness she feared in herself.

If we cannot eventually identify what belongs to us and what to our partner, and thereby reclaim our shadow side and integrate it into ourselves we shall not grow as people, nor will our relationship be based on reality. Our personalities will remain at whatever stage they became stuck in childhood. If couples cannot fulfil each other's needs, then the conflicts of our early life will be perpetuated, for we shall have found in our partner someone who will play the same games of hide and seek as we have played all our lives. Old family patterns of behaviour will eventually re-emerge within us and our own relationships—dominance and submission, punishment and deprivation, aggression and depression, anger and retreat—and we shall forever dance to the same tune, finding security in the familiar:

> Both my 'exs' were the younger of two children and both had elder sisters. Both had great difficulty in communicating emotions though both could show their care for me in letters…
> I disliked the aggression of both. I met my **second** husband at nineteen, married my **first** husband at twenty-two, and married the second one at thirty-five—odd, isn't it?
>
> He divorced. I know he found support and solace from his brothers. One has been married four times and the other three times. I've no idea why they were all so conjugally unstable
>
> COUNSELLOR.

Unless we can change the record.

Angela and Guy

Angela, who had been divorced five years earlier, married Guy, a widower. Her first husband, Jim, had been physically violent to Angela during rows.

Guy and Angela came to counselling, both terrified of what was happening to them after two years of marriage. Guy said Angela 'made him violent', which was, he said, totally contrary to his nature. 'It's as though she expects me to do this,' he said. Angela was driving Guy to react in the way she had always known, for her lack of self-worth led her to feel she deserved this treatment, and the violence she provoked was a form of self-hatred. Angela said she could almost see Jim's presence in the room during confrontations with Guy. What she *really* wanted was an acceptance of the self she could not love. Unable to do this herself, she looked to her partner for it. This set up the reaction of extreme frustration in her partners. In turn Guy's self-esteem plummeted, because of his unwonted lack of control. The couple were in trouble. Angela came to understand the powerful presence of this shadow in her new relationship. She acknowledged that she overreacted to Guy, as she had undoubtedly done to Jim, and put a huge pressure on him which provoked him to frustration and physical fury. She learned to express how she was feeling directly, without eliciting violence.

Why change the habits of a lifetime?

… coming to terms with the unchangeable past, and being able to care for the deprived child in oneself rather than expecting someone else to be the emotional 'horn of plenty'. The alternative is to remain deadlocked in an unsatisfied, but at least familiar, state of feeling badly done by.[3]

The breakup of a relationship, however excruciating at the time, can give us the opportunity to look at the aspects of ourselves, our personalities, and our patterns of action and reaction. The possibility of loving again can be the spur to profound changes in how we behave, if we are prepared to take this risk. Consciously we can opt for someone with whom we can have different expectations of relationship from those models which have not worked for us. Consciously we can ask ourselves what the real basis of our attraction to this person is. The old wounds will still be there, and it will be all to easy to allow ourselves to be channelled into old ways and re-enact earlier scenarios, choose the same partner in a different guise. Maybe we can never be totally transformed, but we *can* modify our behaviour, and we can be aware of how we interact with others, and of their feelings.

It is never up to someone else to dissolve our shadows, to solve our emotional problems, nor to heal our wounds. It is our task and no one else's, though others can enable us by giving us a secure base of love. Good professional counselling or psychotherapy can aid us in shining a torch on our shadow areas and patterns of behaviour, and help us change ways of relating and behaving.

Before we can attempt another relationship, or indeed before we can live at peace with ourselves as single people, we must sort out our responsibility in the breakdown of the previous relationship. One of the keys to making a relationship work is to be aware of the effects of our actions on ourselves, on the relationship and on our partner. But preceding everything must come an understanding of ourselves, our needs, our expectations, our system of relating. Even if our reactions are still those of an infant seeking fusional bliss with a nurturing figure, we must realize that it is neither a sin nor a crime to have these needs and that it is their pursuit to the detriment of all else which is destructive. The needs themselves are normal and can be communicated appropriately—and lovingly.

One of the hardest things in a subsequent relationship is for each partner to accept the shadows from the other's past. Try as we will—and there are some couples who make a pact, tacit or otherwise, not to talk about their previous relationship— something will always arise in the future that will evoke a past memory, and it has to be dealt with:

> *I have lost contact with Charlotte [the first wife]. Yes, it matters a bit but Jancis [the second wife] is not happy about any contact. It's still not easy. Jancis and I do talk to each other, but*

we're thinking of going for relationship counselling. We've put ourselves under a lot of pressure by doing a lot in very little time. It's hard work.

We must bring our whole selves to a relationship, not selected bits, and this must include the past events and people who have shaped and modelled us. We cannot just dismiss a whole period of our lives as though it had no effect on the present. And in a large number of divorces and subsequent relationships the past will always be there, often from both sides, in the form of children and stepchildren, and access rights, and custody. That is unavoidable.

Kelly and Tim

Kelly was thirty-six, and had married Tim after being divorced four years before. Her first marriage had been violent, but she had stayed in it for ten years for fear of admitting her mistake to her family. At thirty-one she had a child, and this had spurred her to leave her first husband. She came to counselling almost afraid to let her new marriage grow and move forward because she was terrified that growth and change would lead to trouble, as in her first marriage. The slightest hint of anything amiss in her life with Tim, instead of being an opportunity to talk through things, froze Kelly in panic because she feared any change could lead to a worse scenario, where violence would once again figure. The shadows from her past came forward each time there was likely to be a breakthrough in communication between her and Tim, and Kelly found it hard to accept that things could go wrong without it leading to a bruising encounter.

Kelly blamed herself for allowing the violence in her first marriage to escalate, but now understands that she could not have changed things in the early days without the life experiences she now has. She acknowledges too how influenced she was by her parents' pressure on her to stay with her first husband. The gradual healing of Kelly's fears and a growing ability to communicate within her relationship has involved confronting her parents and evolving a much more adult way of relating to them. Kelly now says that although 'the shadows will never fully go away' she can more freely express her feelings, and that—for her—it is becoming safe to disagree.

Shadows from the past will always exist, those areas of ourselves that destroy rather than build, and they will re-emerge in all our intimate relationships, even if we were to marry ten times. Patterns will always repeat unless they are resolved.

Resolving them through work done on ourselves is the key not only to being able to make and sustain a loving relationship in the future, but also to letting go of the emotional hold that any previous one has over us. Ideally the time to do this is after the period of intense grieving but before committing ourselves to a new partner. If we see the same phenomena occurring in the new relationship as those that dogged and destroyed our old one then help is needed, and fast, to shine the light of truth on the darkness of our shadows.

1. G. Davis and M. Murch, *Grounds for Divorce*, Clarenden Press 1988, show that 51% of divorced men and 29% of divorced women would have preferred to stay married, and that in 10% of cases both parties wished they had remained married.

2. More than one-third of all current marriages are remarriages for one or both partners. Previously divorced partners are more likely to divorce, and figure in a quarter of all divorces (Source: One plus One).

3. Christopher Clulow and Janet Mattinson, *Marriage Inside Out: Understanding the Problems of Intimacy*, Pelican Books, © The Tavistock Institute of Medical Psychology, 1989, page 156.

12

Forgiveness

The cult of wrongs suffered—negative memory—is a poisoned chalice.[1]

Forgiveness does not pre-empt justice. It recreates; it allows a fresh start. It gives a chance to the neighbour who has wronged us.[2]

Forgiveness, on the face of it, is humanly impossible. Yet forgiveness can be the key to our healing after divorce.

To move on from the place of hurt or guilt, to grow and develop, we must do what, almost invariably, does not come naturally. We must forgive our former spouse, and we must forgive ourselves.

In the death of any human relationship there is rarely an absolute division of sinner and sinned against, though it may sometimes appear so. We on the outside must not judge by appearances. In a marriage which has broken up both partners are to a certain extent both victim and oppressor, however unjust that may sound to the spouse who has been deserted or betrayed.

Oliver and Sandra

Sandra had been a student of eighteen when she met and married Oliver, an academic five years older than she was. Sandra felt inferior among Oliver's friends and colleagues, was constantly trying to please, and tried to shape herself to fit in, even deliberately changing her accent, and agreeing too readily with Oliver, to whom independent thought and intelligence

191

were paramount. Three years into their marriage Oliver fell deeply in love with Jane, a friend of Sandra's, and eventually left Sandra to live with Jane. Finally he and Sandra divorced and he married Jane. To the outsider it would seem that Sandra was an 'innocent' victim of Oliver's infidelity, but in years to come she understood that her very malleability and dependence had contributed to Oliver's falling for someone who was intellectually more robust, and—as Jane herself said—'stubborn'. Sandra, understanding both herself and Oliver, was able to forgive and move on to a new life.

To move on from the experience both must understand and accept their part in everything that caused the breakdown of the marriage, and then give and accept pardon. Yet it is seldom that simple, and certainly never as easy.

What is forgiveness?

I have thought this through so much and I have come to the conclusion that there is no such thing as forgiveness. There is ownership of the truth on both sides, and following that maybe there will be a true expression of sorrow, and then—hopefully— we move on. But who am I to forgive? That would be establishing a hierarchy with one superior to the other.

That was said by a man who had just split up with his partner. He understands that the key to forgiveness is in both sides examining their consciences and understanding why they acted as they did, and the effect this has had on the other. However, it does not fulfil one of the aims of forgiveness which is to enable the other to be free of guilt at failure or wrongdoing, though not of their consequences.

It is perhaps easier to say what forgiveness is not. First of all, it is not forgetting. It would not be possible, nor desirable, to wipe out of our memory any aspect of one of the most significant relationships of our lives. Time may dull the sharpest edge of pain and throw events into a different perspective, but forgiveness is not merely the product of time passing. It is not making excuses for the other, denying our own feelings; it is not wronging ourselves, nor does it necessarily imply the possibility of reconciliation.

Forgiveness is a more positive step which entails recognizing that a bridge has been crossed, that life is for living and that we move on. If we do this then forgiveness will flow naturally, as a by-product of letting go and just getting on. It is unlikely that we shall be able to forgive if we dwell on our hurts, feeding and nurturing them.

In this way forgiveness is freeing ourselves of resentment and of the desire for revenge, it is recognizing the power and the joy that has come when others have forgiven us, it is relieving the other of their moral debt towards us, it is wishing the one who has hurt us well, and thus allowing them the possibility of growth.

Forgiveness has also a sense of foregoing something owed to us. It requires a generosity of spirit which goes hand in hand with the ability to pick up the pieces and move on. Even if we can admit our own failings, perhaps the other cannot see theirs, and we must first be willing to accept that they may never feel able to request forgiveness from us.

Among dictionary[3] definitions of the verb to forgive are 'to cease to feel resentment towards' and 'to *give up* feeling resentment or desire to avenge oneself'. The first is accomplished, if at all, by the passage of time. The second, like true loving (as opposed to being 'in love') depends on an act (or continuous acts) of will. To forgive is consciously to say 'I will no longer be emotionally or morally bound by the hurts which your actions and words have caused me. Yes, some effects will always remain, physical, material and psychological, but I have to deal with those, as you must deal with the issues I have left you with. In forgiving you I am freeing myself to be me, and you to be yourself. You owe me nothing any more, and I will not hang on to the moral power of past wrongs against me, even if *you* can neither apologize nor recognize that there has been a wrong.'

How can we forgive?

My heart is full of bitterness, like a poisoned spring, and my wounds are still open and bleeding. If I forgive it feels like I'm betraying myself, since only revenge can stop me feeling so humiliated. I want to hurt her so until her remorse is as intense as my pain. I'd like to drag her through all the courts so the whole world knows what she has done to me.

To move from these feelings to a place where we can lay down revenge and wish the good of our former partner, to stop pursuing 'justice' and desire mercy, seems a superhuman step, one which during the process of grieving will not usually be possible. Forgiveness is usually the work of the third 'phase' of divorce, the one that follows the intensity of loss. It is a preliminary to moving on—either singly or in a new relationship—and is part of our reintegration into fruitful life. It can happen that when we embark on another relationship the happiness and security we find with a new partner can prompt a generosity of spirit, but ideally forgiveness is part of the work we do on ourselves before we are really free to love again.

The paradox of forgiveness

To be able to forgive is one of those double binds of human existence: we cannot move on until we forgive, but we cannot forgive until we have moved on to a place where we are ready to do so. It is not something which we can force upon ourselves until it is the obvious thing to do. And yet it is an act of will and a conscious decision. We shall know when that moment comes.

It does not come to everybody, and many divorcees will go to their graves embittered by its lack.

The pathway to forgiveness is the work we do on ourselves. Once the loss is assimilated into ourselves and we are well on in the process of mourning the relationship, we can begin to search for the meaning for us in its breakdown. This requires assessing and acknowledging realistically what our responsibility was for its failure. In standing back from the relationship in this way, we are also putting objective distance between us and whatever wrongs may have been done to us and to the marriage.

Forgiving ourselves

We can, if we understand ourselves, move beyond blame and reproach, for we shall know the shadow side of ourselves, and know what are our own traits, views, stances, hopes, fears and expectations and what we have been projecting on to our partner. If we come thus to understand that we have contributed to our partner's suffering in any way, or have created a climate in which the relationship could not grow and be healthy then we may be overcome with a guilt for which it is too late to make reparation. Maybe our sincere expression of sorrow will not be received, still less accepted and reciprocated. We have to live with ourselves; we cannot take back what we have done and are therefore prisoners of ourselves until we can learn to be kind and accept and forgive ourselves. It does not mean making excuses, but looking at the reasons objectively and living with them, and finding in them the seeds of change.

When I understand myself and realize what drives me and channels me into certain courses of action, what holds me back and casts me down, when I know myself and can contemplate myself without judgment but with acceptance and tolerance, then I shall be able to understand other people, and from there it is a short step to full forgiveness. Often it is not possible to know ourselves to this extent without skilled help. One woman said that it was not until she applied to train as a counsellor and underwent a basic grounding in psychology that she came to know *herself*, and went on from there to understand or forgive actions in the past which had hurt her. It was a significant step, she said, in forgiving herself, and thus being free to be herself.

To understand ourselves we need to look at:

■ the shadows, the patterns of our behaviour, where they came from;

■ what happened in early life that contributed to our relational difficulties;

■ how much we really wanted to change;

■ how flexible we were;

■ how complacent we were;

■ what our expectations of the relationship were;

■ whether we were better at blaming rather than communicating;

■ whether we were able to back down;

■ how good a listener we were;

■ how much time we gave to building the relationship.

It is so easy to blame the other until we start answering these questions honestly. But, as in the parable of the man who had a large plank of wood in his eye yet was busy pointing out the speck of dust in the other chap's eye[4], if we cannot look at our own responsibility then we shall stay isolated, unable to interrelate on any realistic level.

Once we have looked at ourselves in the light of truth, then the healing process of forgiveness can begin: neither a grudging hypocritical forgiveness of our partner, nor condescension concerning the offences which in truth it took two to commit, nor an anguished guilty remorse-laden beating of our own breast, nor yet complacency.

1. Paul Oestreicher, *The Tablet*, June 21, 1997.
2. Jacques Gaillot, former bishop of Evreux, sacked by the Vatican in January 1995.
3. *Longman Dictionary of the English Language*, first printed 1984.
4. From the Gospel according to Luke, chapter 6 verses 42-43.

13

Moving on

Pain is the nitty-gritty of divorce, but also hope and resurrection.
JACK DOMINIAN

Is divorce the life sentence that some feel it to be? Is it possible for *everyone* to take control, and emerge from their personal prison of grief into something more fulfilling and productive?

The beginning of the rest of our lives?

When we divorce we are forced, if only by practical circumstances, into change, to pass from our former married life to a new set of circumstances. Divorce means perforce a shift from one life structure to another. The old one is past, however much we miss it; or we terminate it, however regrettable that may be. Divorce, whether welcome or a cruel blow, *is* 'the beginning of the rest of our lives'.

What the rest of our lives will be depends now on us. It will be influenced, as we have seen, by many factors:

- the extent of the loss experienced;

- whether we have suffered other significant losses in our lives;

- a whole set of material circumstances;

- what sort of support network we have;

- whether we are challenged as well as supported;

- whether we generally esteem and accept ourselves;

- whether we are sufficiently autonomous as people to cope with being alone;

- our personal value system and/or faith.

Somehow, in the welter of emotion, financial problems, legal hassles, upset and disturbed children, in the jumble of a strange, disjointed world, we have to move on into the possibility of new living. Depending on our general outlook on life it will sound either realistic or trite and unjust to say that it is in pain that we learn most, that we are most open to change, provided that we do not pull up the protective drawbridge and cut ourselves off from life. It is nonetheless true, and those who have been through pain and come out the other side will testify to its truth, often saying that they would not have been without the experience. Our personal crucifixion can lead to a glorious resurrection, and pain can be converted into energy:

There is something to be said for it... I've got to use this in what I do. I can transform it, or transfer it, or transmogrify it into something better. I've got to get it out. All I can do is to draw some deeper meaning out of it, out of the experience, express it at some other level. That sounds very grand! But you must transform it by a creative act of some sort. If you can do something like that with the heartache, even if it's only one per cent success, it's creative energy...

The challenge of divorce, and of all passages and transitions of human life, is to move on, assimilating and subsuming the good, and understanding and learning from the bad.

Support and values

Our response to being divorced, and what we make of life post-divorce, will depend heavily on the support and challenge available in our personal environment and the inner strength we have, or can find.

- Are we just going to give in and stay stuck in grief and bitterness?

- Is there help available?

- Can we take control of our lives and find the help we need?

- Where do we find the values which will help us change?

Each of us must answer these questions for ourselves.

Friends

We have seen in Chapter 7 that we may lose friends at the same time as we lose our spouse and possibly also our children and home. But new friends are always there for the making, and true friends do not abandon us. It is up to us not to be a drag and demand too much of their time and energy, and also up to us to remember that a real friend is someone who loves us sufficiently to be truthful, and will tell us honestly where we are going wrong.

If we are the one to befriend someone who is suffering loss of any kind we must be sure that we do not offer more than we can deliver, for we need to be reliable. We also need to put in 'boundaries' and make it clear that we are not infinitely available and that we have areas of our own lives which need time and attention. Within these parameters we can offer support and acceptance, companionship and challenge—but never advice, for if we do we can end up taking blame and responsibility. To help our divorcing friends, we should:

- accept their feelings and not hurry them out of these too soon ('You've cried enough now' is unhelpful);

- 'hold' them until the pain has subsided sufficiently for them to unpack the reasons for the split;

- help and support them in 'owning' their pain and misery;

- understand we can't make it come right for them;

- be sensitive to the moment where they may be ready to let go and move forward;

- help and support them in learning new skills, developing their strengths, making plans, assessing and taking risks as they venture into new territory;

- build up their self-esteem;

- be trustworthy.

Values

Values give us a sense of purpose and, from that, dignity and worth; they root our existence in something beyond the present moment. They give us principles which enable us to establish the priorities of our lives. If we live by them, they enable us to change. Values can come from our religious faith or spirituality, our beliefs (for example, caring for the environment), our ethnic or cultural background, our education, or quite simply the human values which we absorb in counselling, group therapy, clubs, classes, aerobics. Values thus go hand in hand with belonging.

Belonging is one of the keys to healing after one of life's painful transitions, for we gain strength and support from somewhere where we can be accepted for ourselves—whether this is family, group, community or church. In belonging we can turn our gaze off ourselves and our troubles, while at the same time being surrounded and supported.

Rebuilding ourselves

I've survived. I've moved on. I've learned about myself.

It is a common experience during divorce and the period of grieving that we feel that some essential part of ourselves does not exist. Something vital to our perception of ourselves has been attacked, and we may believe it to have been destroyed for ever. To start to rebuild that most essential 'us' we must stop projecting our anger and guilt and sorrow on to our former partner, own our feelings (this is the process of forgiveness of self and of the other person dealt with in Chapter 12), and learn to live with emotions which may fluctuate and be ambivalent. Bowlby[1], in his work on loss, reduced the process of grieving to its simplest terms: the increasingly accurate processing of information. As the reality of the breakup, and the facts of our new state, become part of ourselves and our existence, then a sense of control of our own lives will start gradually to seep back into our daily life.

As we begin to rebuild, to understand ourselves and the other person, and to forgive, we move through the stages described in the process of Transactional Analysis[2]:

- Anger: 'I'm OK—you're not OK.'

- Guilt: 'I'm not OK—you're OK.'

to

- Acceptance and tolerance: 'I'm OK—you're OK.'

We—my 'ex' and I—are both OK, are understood and forgiven, which means I am OK enough to start building for the future. Time is of little consequence in becoming sufficiently 'OK' to let go and move on; it is the work we do on ourselves that counts. Even then, progress in rebuilding ourselves is never smooth. One counsellor said:

Being OK is not having made it, but having your hand over the edge. There will constantly be a slipping back.

As throughout all our human journey, it is this process of rebuilding which is more important than the finished edifice.

Self-esteem

The things you do, you do to make yourself feel better.

Self-esteem, or the lack of it, or its death at the hands of our spouse, has recurred like a leitmotiv throughout this book. Again the whole area of self-esteem is one of human nature's great double binds. Those whose idea of their own value is lowest are the most likely to select partners who will collude with them in their belief:

What attracted him to me in the first place was that he was prepared to take me on.

These people will unconsciously select mates who turn out to be dominating and controlling, allowing no space for the building up of their spouse's personality, and the ultimate failure of the marriage will be the culmination of all the damaging blows to self-worth that those who suffer from low self-esteem collect like trophies.

During the termination of a marriage, our very self is attacked till we do not feel we exist any more; our identity has gone. We have to cling on to what this counsellor said:

It is the relationship which has failed, not you.

Low self-esteem can erode a relationship like nothing else: we will test because we cannot trust; we belittle in order to make ourselves feel bigger; we are jealous, demanding, possessive because we want proofs of the love of which we believe we are unworthy. Not existing in our own right, we shall be negative and constantly inward-looking, wanting to suck into ourselves as much love as possible in order to exist. Low self-esteem wants to get love, and has nothing to give. If we seek to boost our shattered or non-existent sense of worth (to prove we are 'OK') with a relationship too quickly after separation or divorce we are unlikely to be able to create or sustain a mature relationship. However, without another to bolster up our sense of self we shall remain in a negative slough of despond:

I had developed feelings that were more than simply friendly. The main effect… was to build my self-esteem, so badly damaged by the loss of my husband to what turned out to be not one, but two, other women. I started to like myself again because he, a young and glamorous person, so obviously liked me and kept saying so. For months after he had left I still felt good about myself. But I was not aware that that renewal of my self-esteem was, in a sense, based on his bestowal of it, and in discovering that he did not want me as a lover, I suffered a huge lowering of self-esteem all over again.

The seven deadly sayings…

If we sincerely wish to work on ourselves, these are mindsets[3] to eliminate:

- 'It always happens'—we see a one-off negative event as part of a never-ending series of failures.

- 'If I sense it, it's true'—ignoring the facts, we guess at another person's reaction to us.

- 'If only I hadn't done/said that'—we feel responsible for causing a problem—even though it may have had complex causes—and thus guilty, reiterating our internal dialogue of 'shoulds' and 'oughts'.

■ 'It's no good'—if one thing goes wrong in a relationship or a task we are carrying out, we dwell on that and ignore any positive elements.

■ 'It doesn't count'—we decry our successes and play down the positive.

■ 'I've got to be perfect'—we demand superhuman achievement of ourselves in relationships and work. Anything less is worthless.

■ 'I'm not intelligent/attractive/good'—we transform one bad experience into a universal truth that destroys optimism, paralyses us and prevents any initiative.

In order to start to live again, singly or with a new partner, we must first become ourselves and believe that self to be good. For someone who now recognizes that their self-esteem has never been high, and has explored the past to discover why, therapy or skilled counselling will probably be needed to achieve some sense of self-worth. For others, whose value in their own eyes has been temporarily battered by guilt, failure, betrayal or desertion, it is possible to work these issues through with the help of good friends.

But there is no substitute for getting on with living, working, daily being. Our job can give a feeling of being wanted and valued; our parenting skills—even if we cannot always see this—give us a reason for pride in our achievements. Self-help books suggest how we can come to believe in ourselves, and the newsagents' shelves are full of magazines suggesting that evening classes, car mechanics, a health hydro or circuit training are the answer. By themselves they are not, but the attitude that goes out to tackle these things is half the battle, and a new competence will add to our worth in our own eyes.

The following letter was written by one of the interviewees

who contributed to this book (details are changed):

You might be interested to know that within about a month of talking to you I succeeded in finding a job as an assistant in a publishing firm. Although I had not planned to work full-time, I am finding it fascinating and extremely educational. The new environment is stimulating in many ways, and the way office life works and Cambridge life works is endlessly absorbing. I am significantly happier than I was when I saw you, and I think it is definitely part of emotional healing to be accepted as my new self—i.e. middle-aged and single, and welcomed as being valuable.

Health

Mind and body are part of the same entity, the human being. If we feel better in one area we shall feel better all over, and physical fitness really does help us to pull through. It is all part of valuing ourselves sufficiently to eat nourishing foods, to cook interesting meals, to get enough sleep and to look after our bodies. It is a significant step towards self-esteem.

We have seen from statistics that divorcees, especially men, drink and smoke more than their married counterparts. Similarly, there is a heavy reliance on anti-depressants, with the majority of research interviewees having been on medication of this sort at some point, sometimes for years. In some instances drugs can hold up the grieving process, though they do dull the pain. One counsellor, who works with many divorcing and separated people, said:

So many clients are on medication. Doctors are very willing to give anti-depressants to patients going through divorce, but it really does affect the work they may do on themselves, with or without a counsellor. They slow the reaction to everything, and prevent them owning their emotions. I find there is an incongruence in their body language. I am not seeing the real them. It is very common.

We must learn to answer these questions:

- What areas of my life need setting right?
- What stops me getting the best from each day?
- What is missing in order to be happy?

The answer is not 'someone to love me', nor is it anything on the outside of ourselves.

A counsellor said:

Always look back and see what you have accomplished—rather than groaning under the burden of what still needs to be done.

When we can live the present moment to the best of our ability, and not look either back with negative 'if onlys' or forward with fear, we shall be someone in our own right with a knowledge of who and what we are.

For four years I have scarcely opened a book, and there have been times of intense fatigue. I've been lonely, especially when my mother died. But my driving aim was to keep going. After that period of solitude I gained a great deal—I have widened the field of possibilities in my life, and I have discovered potential in me that I never suspected. I've also gained in confidence and security.

DIVORCED MOTHER OF FOUR

Being single

*I've become a stronger person since I've been on my own. I think
I lived in his shadow rather.*

The freedom for which, as married people, we may yearn can
become something of which we cannot or do not know how to
take advantage, something which weighs heavily—a source of
anguish. We can experience boredom, sadness at not being able
to share experiences and feelings at a profound level, difficulty at
having to solve practical problems or make major decisions
alone, with no one to lean on, or creating a satisfying social life.
Sundays and public holidays—Christmas especially—can be
hell. We feel incomplete, and perhaps in some way second-class.

We tend to ignore that this same freedom offers us many
advantages, even luxuries—coming and going as we please,
eating when the mood takes us, watching TV when we please,
growing a beard for a few days, taking time out for ourselves,
and meeting whom we want when we want. Away from a tense
relationship our self-esteem and confidence may grow naturally.

Being single requires different skills from those which we
need for living in a family or couple unit. These can be learned
and assimilated, and the proof is that many single, separated,
widowed or divorced people lead happy and fulfilled lives.
Those at ease with singleness, whether for them it is temporary
or permanent, are able to live fully for the moment rather than
scanning the future horizon for a potential partner to rescue
them from the prison of loneliness. They have many interests,
many friends, are active in organizing their evenings, weekends
and holidays—as well as enjoying time spent alone.

Hard though it may seem to those in the throes of loneliness for
the first time in their lives, we must remember that we can all work
towards our own happiness, and that it does not depend on anyone
else. Other people—friends, colleagues, a lover or a spouse—may
enhance it or detract from it, but we are responsible for it.

Being a single parent

Studies comparing children from broken and intact homes show that children of divorced parents show more delinquency, are expelled from school more frequently, and their exam record is poorer than their peers from two-parent households. Later they become sexually active younger, with more teen pregnancies. They marry and divorce earlier and more frequently. These family systems produce sad cycles of emotional deprivation which can last for generations:

This will go on till I die. It will probably go on till my children die because it's cyclical.

Being a single parent magnifies all the already-demanding tasks of parenthood. Becoming a single parent overnight will require reserves of strength, and a great deal of extra loving for children who are stressed, confused and traumatized at a time when it is hard enough to keep going ourselves. Further down the line there will be quite an intense pressure to cope with everything better in order to prove that problems cannot be blamed on being a divorced lone parent.

Every child needs love and security, but also boundaries and discipline, and when our feelings about ourselves are at a low ebb, when we are torn and angry it is hard to provide those things for our children when they most need them. The better we feel about ourselves, the better we shall relate to our children.

We shall, inevitably, have bad days—when we take out our negativity, pain and despair on our children. It helps to acknowledge this to them and apologize, which means neither that we are failures, nor that we are burdening them with adult problems if we simply say we are sorry and add the reason—stress at work, or an unexpectedly large bill, for example. Never, however, must we draw them into any continuing conflictual interplay between us and our former spouse.

Here is where mediation[4] comes into its own, for by this means divorcing parents can be helped to agree with a minimum of bitterness and rancour on issues concerning children. If at all possible a divorcing couple should negotiate a common way of parenting their children, so that there is as little discrepancy as possible in discipline—bedtime, pocket money, amount of TV watched, and so that they cannot play one parent off against the other.

However gutted we may be feeling, we must understand that our children will also be going through a difficult time, missing the other parent, or having to adapt to seeing that parent, or us, with a new partner. They will be insecure, and this may show in work and attitude, and we must make time to listen to them and respond accurately to their needs and emotions. If possible, and they are old enough, we can 'empower' our children by making them part of the decision-making processes of the household, and yet making sure they still understand that we are in charge.

Children will often cling on to the fantasy that their parents' relationship can be restored, and this notion—together with the emotional upheaval they go through—may cause them to create often terminal difficulties in any subsequent relationships their parents may initiate. Jack Dominian warns:

Children are notorious for creating hell in second relationships. They are a potent factor in their failure.

Seeing our former partner

I do see him. I don't know whether I should. He came down at the bank holiday. I talk to him on the phone. He wants to help. I don't see myself as his partner any more.

Sometimes we are forced to see our former partner because we live in the same town or they collect the children, or for whatever reason. Sometimes we are obliged to see the partner we still yearn to belong to with someone else. The wounds of rejection and betrayal, guilt and failure, separation and divorce are constantly reopened and bleed.

Sometimes, if we still nurse hopes that reconciliation is possible, at the 'bargaining' stage of grief, we ask to be friends with the man or woman whose bed we have shared and whose children we too have parented. It is not ultimately impossible for what was once intimate, indeed passionate, love to turn into friendship, but it depends on having fully mourned the relationship, on having first been reconciled with ourselves and having forgiven our spouse.

If we try too quickly to make a conjugal relationship into one of friendship we shall find ourselves slipping back into the old patterns of relating which brought about the breakdown of the relationship. Our energies are better employed working on ourselves and discovering new friends.

From time to time we may have a desperate urge to contact our spouse, to try once more to revive what is dead and gone. We must understand and accept the desire without necessarily giving in to it, and perhaps ask a close friend or family member or counsellor to help us continue the mourning process. It requires strength of mind and purpose, but it becomes easier with practice.

There are, of course, couples who remarry each other. If this is the result of a deeper understanding of themselves, their partner and their needs—rather than the comfort of habit— then there will be a greater chance of success second time round:

We remarried again because she wanted another child and we thought it should be born in wedlock. Our second marriage was probably doomed because we had never even discussed the reasons for the first breakup. I was devastated when it finally ended. She just said: 'I don't love you any more and I want you to go.'[5]

Being a couple

It is a commonplace to say that so often we rush into a fresh relationship without having sorted out the old one, and that this can lead to the same patterns, behaviours and problems recurring. If it is said so often it is because it is a frequent occurrence, and one which goes a long way to explaining the rapid failure of so many second marriages. And if we are already in a new relationship when the separation and divorce occur there is probably a fair amount of denial on our own part about the causes of the marital breakdown, which almost certainly will have repercussions on the new partnership.

Many people are unable to spend time on their own, and will leave one relationship only when they know there is another to go to, or else they immediately seek a new partner. In either case there will not have been time for the working through and grieving that is necessary when so important a part of our lives ends.

If we are hunting, consciously or not, for someone to rescue us from single solitude, someone to bolster up our punctured self-image, we shall not be our true selves; we shall be creatures who are willing to compromise on that self in order to get love. Beware: 'I need you' does not mean: 'I love you.' There is no way that is less likely to sustain a lasting and loving relationship of equals. But similarly we must not set ourselves up as invulnerable, protecting ourselves to the exclusion of warmth and trust against possible hurt and disappointment.

During our time of solitude when we are without a lover or a partner, we must try to get our needs met in other ways—or meet them ourselves. If we look to a new partner for all our emotional hunger to be sated then we shall set impossible standards, and our disappointment will be correspondingly more crushing. We shall never be satisfied by the love of someone else until we can love ourselves, and to do that we need to know ourselves, our patterns of relating, and what we need and hope for from a relationship:

I think I grew an enormous amount personally as a result. I learned a lot about myself and about relationships. Experiencing that degree of pain has made me stronger as an individual. In a way I'm glad it's happened because I learned things about myself I would not otherwise have done—and about marriage. I do see myself as a better husband. I am more aware of what I'm doing. I listen more. It is difficult to change old behaviour patterns, but I am changing them, I think.

Our future is ours to construct, but we do this by living in the present, each day for what it brings and what we can give. When we can do this we may or may not choose to share it with someone else.

1. John Bowlby: *Attachment and Loss Volume 1: Attachment, Attachment and Loss Volume 2: Separation: Anger and Anxiety, Attachment and Loss: Volume 3: Loss: Sadness and Depression,* Penguin Books, © The Tavistock Institute of Human Relations, 1980.
2. *I'm OK—You're OK,* Thomas A. Harris M.D., © Thomas Harris M.D., 1967, 1968, 1969, published by Arrow Books in 1995.
3. Formulated by Dr Aaron Beck, one of the founders of cognitive therapy in the 1960s at the University of Pennsylvania.
4. See Appendix 1 on the Family Law Act 1996 and mediation.
5. 'Can't live with you—or without you' by Toby Harnden, *Daily Telegraph,* 17 November 1994.

CONCLUSION

A rite of passage for our times?

'...power comes to its full strength in weakness... for when I am weak, then am I strong.'[1]

The purpose of this book has not been to give recipes for the prevention of marriage breakdown. Pundits will advocate better preparation for wedlock; tuition in how to argue; multiple-choice questionnaires for computer analysis to see if partners are well-matched; support at the critical phases of the union— the birth of the first child, beginning school, adolescence, children's departure, retirement. The government, in an attempt to stem the estimated £3.4 billion (some say higher) annual cost of divorce, decided in 1997 to spend half a million pounds on marriage preparation, telephone counselling, drop-in centres and marriage support help lines.

It would be naïve to believe that, in the short-term, any of this will do much to cut the divorce rate. Society in the United Kingdom at the millennium has gone a long way beyond immediate help, and it will take many generations to undo the damage to marriage. It may be that our ideal of stable monogamy will never return. Dysfunctional systems of relating have their roots deep in childhood and infancy, and are learned young, and today's children—and their children—will have few role models on which to base their marriages. Not every marriage can survive, for sometimes our wounds are too deep, our capacity for love too limited, our expectations of fulfilment too high, our stresses too crushing.

Divorce is inevitable in some cases, and this book has endeavoured to deal with this fact.

Taking account of the inescapable fact of divorce, the aim was to map out its consequences in an attempt to reduce the feeling of isolation and entrapment in pain for those going through it, and to help those standing on the sidelines to support them effectively and non-judgmentally.

During the final stages of writing came the news of the death of Diana, Princess of Wales. It was followed by a collective and engulfing outpouring of emotion, which maybe reveals how bruised and hurt our society has become. The multiplicity of media images showing her cradling the sick, the broken and the dying seemed to express the need in all of us to be loved and held, without judgment, without censure. One of the intentions of this book is to show exactly what the ravages of divorce are on an individual, and to ask those who surround them to show understanding and compassion.

It has tried, above all, to give a realistic and contemporary picture, and avoid being trite and simplistic, for we have been writing about human tragedy, the life sentence which is divorce.

But life implies living and opportunity, and not the death of hope. For this reason the final section of the book was devoted to the more positive possibilities which are opened up to us by divorce: those of self-knowledge, of changing old patterns, of increased autonomy and of fulfilment. But so many divorcees seem shackled by bitterness, self-doubt and pessimism.

The overwhelming and negative feeling of many divorcees—that they had rather their partner had died, and that death would have been easier to cope with—could perhaps be turned round. The hope that exists while our partner lives on is not of getting back together and restoring an unviable relationship, but of finishing unfinished business, of understanding the problems and patterns, forgiving the wrongs, and establishing a new (if distant) way of relating which leaves both with feelings of dignity and worth, and which can give any children of the marriage a pattern of honesty, civility, decorum, of working through difficult issues, and of honesty and conciliation.

In divorce we need a way of ending which produces these results, for a well-managed ending leaves individuals feeling in control and able to cope. So often those who divorce have already undergone difficult life experiences, and are lacking in self-worth. A good ending to a bad relationship allows us to see that there is another way, and that even this disaster is redeemable.

And so the conclusion became evident during the course of research and writing that it is the way that the ending of the marriage is handled that will have a long-term effect on all the parties concerned, though primarily on the ex-partners and their children. Once the decision to divorce is taken—for whatever reason, it is the *how*, as well as the why, that is important.

It will not always be possible, in the teeth of hurt or betrayal, to open out a discussion of the breakup well in advance of separation, or to recognize the problems posed by dependency (emotional and financial), nor will it be likely for us to work out some sort of agreement by ourselves, nor to acknowledge the other's feelings of anger, despair, fear and confusion when our own may be blinding us. Because of our human failings and fragility we all to some extent have difficulty facing up to endings that are final, and we will put up resistance to anything which forces us to do so in any structured and formal way.

Mediation, although this is not one of its primary objectives, can provide just such a formalized (even solemnized) ending in that it involves (as does courtship) meeting, communication, dialogue, agreement and commitment to future action. As in all things, the process is of vital importance, and in this case may precede the forgiveness which is the true sign of having loved, lost and grown in the process.

We have noted at several points in this book that divorce lacks any ritual to mark it as a status passage. Human beings need rites of passage to signal endings and beginnings, to bridge critical stages in their life process. Not so long ago (and for some, still) religion provided rituals of 'hatch, match and dispatch'—baptism or circumcision, the churching of women after childbirth, initiation into the adult world at adolescence (confirmation, bar mitzvah), nuptial celebrations, and of course funerals after death.

The aim of these ceremonies was not only to mark the transition from one stage of life to another for the individuals concerned, but also to give public formalization of the event. These rites maintained the social order, and reiterated society's investment in the people making the transition, and their reciprocal contribution to the social order. The secularization of society has either eliminated these or reduced them to a minimum, and with them we have lost much which gave meaning to these times of transition, and which helped relieve stress at times of great emotional, psychological and practical rearrangement. It is worth noting that almost always these rites of passage incorporated non-verbal symbolism (water, cutting, oil, rings, burial).

In divorce, which is an unscheduled and often chaotic breach of the social order, there is no such ritual, save a possible appearance in court. There is no symbolic severing from the old status or adjustment to the new. One of the principle consequences of this lack is that we retain the concept of *failure* when our marriage ends, instead of seeing it more positively as *change*.

In Chapter 10 we mentioned that the United Reformed Church has a service for release from vows, in which sorrow and regret are expressed, before either partner can move on to remarry in church after divorce. It is manifestly not possible or desirable to impose any formula, still less a religious one, on all parting couples. It would seem, though, that the new divorce procedures under the 1996 Family Law Act[2], with their opportunities for husband and wife to meet in a safe, non-threatening environment with an impartial mediator, and in order to find and agree options for the practical arrangements of parting, could provide a forum for some sort of formalized parting. The couple, having had their feelings heard and acknowledged, and having worked out practical solutions, could—before the divorce is definitively pronounced—have a final meeting with the mediator, in which there is some kind of conclusion, and, if desired, a return of the rings exchanged at matrimony, or some other token that had been vested with symbolic value within the relationship.

This would be a simple and brief formalization of regret and no return, freeing both former partners to grieve fully and healthily without becoming stuck in recrimination and bitterness. It would give the 'losing' partner some sense of equality and dignity, and prevent the 'leaving' spouse denying the reality of the breakup, and offer them a chance to express regret at the situation. Both might emerge with more of a sense of completion, of an exchange, of the possibility of rebirth into a different way of living, than the stark impersonality of a decree absolute.

It will not take the sting out of the reality, nor is it simply a question of emotional damage limitation, but of freeing us to be ourselves, to embark on a time of transformation before, as van Gennep[3] says, we can 'begin acting again, but in a different way'.

1. 2 Corinthians chapter 12 verses 9 and 10.
2. See Appendix 1 on the 1996 Family Law Act.
3. Arnold van Gennep, *Les Rites de Passage* (*The Rites of Passage*), E. Nourry, Paris, 1907, and Routledge and Kegan Paul, London.

APPENDIX 1

The Family Law Act 1996— the new legislation explained

Marriage is an important and long-established institution that provides most people with a supportive and loving relationship to take them through life. It also provides a strong framework for the rearing of children. The Government is committed to supporting marriage. However, while couples enter marriage intending it to be for life, some reach a point when they feel that they can no longer continue in the marriage. Where this is the case, the Government's objective has been to put in place divorce laws that enable couples to consider fully whether they really want a divorce, and if they do, to focus on the consequences of divorce before it is granted. The overall objective remains to support marriage wherever possible, and to ensure that couples have full information on the options available to them before reaching a decision to divorce.

LORD CHANCELLOR'S DEPARTMENT, MARRIAGE AND THE FAMILY LAW ACT 1996.

The legislation which was passed in the summer of 1996 aimed to put an end to a system which allowed people permanently to break up their marriages within as little as three months, if 'fault' were alleged. The previous divorce act was considered damaging to marriages, for it allowed little thinking through of the consequences of divorce, and emphasized the divisions between the couple rather than attempting to save their relationship.

The Family Law Act stipulates a period of reflection and consideration which will give couples an opportunity to consider whether divorce is really what they want, and to make all the practical arrangements (primarily for their children, but also for finance and accommodation) before the divorce is granted. There will be no grounds of a fault, which was previously necessary to obtain a 'quickie' divorce.

The reflection period will normally be twelve months, but can be extended to eighteen months if there are children under sixteen, or if one partner requests this extra time.

When one or both partners declare a wish to divorce they must now attend a one-to-one information meeting which will give them full details of what divorce entails, and lets them know what options are open to them. Then, after three months' 'cooling off', during which they will be encouraged to attend a marriage counselling session (free for those on legal aid), one or both of them make a 'statement of marital breakdown', indicating that one or both:

- believe the marriage has broken down;

- understand the purpose of the period for reflection and consideration;

- wish to make arrangements for the future.

Following receipt of this statement by the court there will follow a nine-month period for reflection and consideration, during which the couple could:

- reflect on whether their marriage can be saved;

- have the opportunity to be reconciled;

- consider what arrangements regarding finance, property and children should be made for the future.

Together with the time between the information meeting and the statement of breakdown, this means a minimum wait of a year before one of the parties can apply for a divorce. At the end of this period, an application for a divorce or separation order may be made to the court. This application would be accompanied by a declaration to the effect that, having reflected on the breakdown of the marriage and considered the arrangements for the future, the party or parties involved believe that the marriage cannot be saved. (For a summary of the whole process, see the diagram on page 222.)

What does not change in this Act is the bar on divorcing within the first year of marriage.

Information meetings

These are intended to be for the couple or an individual, and should provide relevant information concerning:

- marriage support services;

- the importance of the welfare, wishes and feelings of the children;

- the protection available against violence, and how to obtain support and assistance;

- the type of financial issues which might arise following divorce or separation;

- the availability of independent legal advice and representation;

- the legal aid scheme;

- the divorce process and parties' responsibilities and rights under it;

- the availability and advantages of mediation.

STAGES IN THE NEW DIVORCE PROCESS

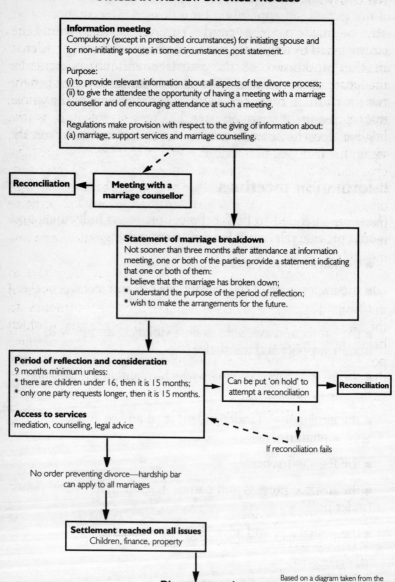

Information meeting
Compulsory (except in prescribed circumstances) for initiating spouse and for non-initiating spouse in some circumstances post statement.

Purpose:
(i) to provide relevant information about all aspects of the divorce process;
(ii) to give the attendee the opportunity of having a meeting with a marriage counsellor and of encouraging attendance at such a meeting.

Regulations make provision with respect to the giving of information about:
(a) marriage, support services and marriage counselling.

Reconciliation

Meeting with a marriage counsellor

Statement of marriage breakdown
Not sooner than three months after attendance at information meeting, one or both of the parties provide a statement indicating that one or both of them:
* believe that the marriage has broken down;
* understand the purpose of the period of reflection;
* wish to make the arrangements for the future.

Period of reflection and consideration
9 months minimum unless:
* there are children under 16, then it is 15 months;
* only one party requests longer, then it is 15 months.

Access to services
mediation, counselling, legal advice

Can be put 'on hold' to attempt a reconciliation

Reconciliation

If reconciliation fails

No order preventing divorce—hardship bar can apply to all marriages

Settlement reached on all issues
Children, finance, property

Divorce granted

Based on a diagram taken from the
Marriage Care Annual Report 1996

Mediation[1]

Mediation is a process whereby an impartial negotiator helps couples considering a divorce to meet and discuss in order to deal with the practical arrangements which must be made for the future. Because this is a face-to-face negotiation between the two parties, a mediator can more readily identify those marriages which might be saved than can solicitors whose litigious processes keep a couple apart and bitter. It was the view of several counsellors that some people will use the legal channels as a kind of test to see if their marriage is really ended. But when they get embroiled in the adversarial system, they often find no way out. One divorcing barrister, who went to mediation with his wife of twenty-one years, said it helped resolve the things which in a solicitor's letter would 'send one into orbit'.[2]

Mediation focuses the couple on the decisions they have to take, and its methods spring from the arbitration processes of industrial disputes rather than from counselling techniques. In the end it is the couple's capacity to reach an agreement which helps them most, whatever the issues in dispute. It is usually a positive process because it improves communication between the spouses, helping them say even extremely painful things to each other.

The tasks of the mediator are these:

- to explain the process;

- to identify issues;

- to explore these;

- to generate options;

- to help reach a settlement or define where the disagreement is.

Unlike the adversarial legal route, mediation can ease the

burden of separation by focusing on reducing conflict and making sure that the needs of the children are heard, thus lessening the damage on young lives.

It can, in its way, help the healing process—something which will scarcely have begun, so raw may be the feelings of one or both partners. Often where one spouse has left the home to live with someone else, the one who is left behind can be raw, bitter and angry and may try to block the settlement of vital issues as a means of getting their own back or exercising power. But through mediation the 'weaker' partner can contribute to the decisions made; their voice is heard, and this can go some way to building self-esteem, which is the vital ingredient for starting to live again.

Mediation is about short-term management of problems, leading to long-term coping.

Roland and Angela

Roland and Angela came to mediation in a bad way. Roland was depressed, resentful and hurt since Angela had requested a divorce, and she in her turn was feeling guilty about her decision to leave the marriage. She showed this by trying to be 'caring', to which Roland responded by being increasingly bitter. The mediator was able to discern that Roland felt that the bottom had fallen out of his life and that he was losing everything, and she acknowledged his feelings. Roland's relief at having his feelings understood and accepted was palpable. In turn the mediator helped Angela to grasp that she needed to say things to Roland about what, in fact, he was retaining— both materially and in terms of contact with the children— and her good opinion of him as a father.

A mediator can therefore help a warring couple say things to each other which promote their feelings of value as people, even if their role as a spouse is over. By giving them both control over decisions and enabling them to develop plans, for example, for joint (though separate) parenting, and by facilitating problem-solving, the mediator will greatly enhance their sense of worth at a time when all too often pain, remorse, guilt and anger drown all positive feelings.

1. I am indebted to Thelma Fisher, Director of National Family Mediation, for the information on mediation in this section.
2. 'How James and Theresa stopped fighting with help from Mary and Jacqueline', by Cassandra Jardine, *Daily Telegraph*, 28 April, 1995.

APPENDIX 2

The stages of loss—theories

There are many theories of how people come to terms with loss, and these generally hold good for any loss—whether of a person or a relationship (through death or divorce), an animal, a job, a place, a treasured possession. All ultimately reflect **van Gennep**'s[1] observation of the structure of the universal rite of passage:

- separation;

- transition;

- incorporation.

One of the best known theories is that of **Elisabeth Kübler-Ross**[2], whose seminars at the University of Chicago were initiated to help consider the implications of terminal illness for dying patients and those involved in their care, which enabled many to identify and come to terms with their own feelings and to respond constructively. Dr Kübler-Ross postulated six stages through which a terminally ill person can progress before they can die peacefully and with full acceptance. Often the dying for a variety of reasons—and especially if help is not forthcoming—stick at one or other stage, and so may die isolated, angry, bitter or depressed.

According to Kübler-Ross's observations the stages (or sets of emotions) of the psycho-emotional process of the 'loss' of one's own life are these:

- denial and isolation;

- anger ;

- bargaining;

- depression;
- acceptance;
- hope.

Kübler-Ross's observations have been summarized and added to by **Elizabeth Collick**[3], who uses phrases to illustrate the sets of emotions experienced. The first few especially will be familiar to those whose marital breakup came without warning:

- shock: 'I just went cold';
- numbness and unreality: 'This isn't me';
- disbelief: 'It can't be true';
- yearning: 'Come back';
- emptiness: 'An aching void';
- searching: 'He must be somewhere';
- anxiety: 'Must I sell the house?';
- anger: 'He had no right to leave me like this';
- guilt: 'If only...';
- remembering: 'I'm afraid of forgetting';
- depression: 'I'm too tired to bother';
- loss of identity and status: 'Who am I?';
- stigma: 'I'm an embarrassment to others';
- sexual deprivation: 'To have a man's arms around me';
- loss of faith: 'Why?';
- loneliness: 'I just dread weekends';
- acceptance: 'He'd have laughed about it';
- healing.

Another theorist whose trilogy of works on attachment and loss are seminal is **John Bowlby**[4]. Bowlby studied the response of young children to the temporary or permanent loss of a mother figure, and the expressions of anxiety, grief and mourning which accompany such loss. From this Bowlby evolved his concept of the stages of mourning, and applied them to adults. They are:

- phase of numbing, lasting usually only a few hours up to a week, and can be interrupted by outbursts of intense distress and/or anger;

- phase of yearning and searching for the lost figure lasting some months and sometimes years;

- phase of disorganization and despair;

- phase of [more or less] reorganization.

Bowlby noted that adult response to loss sometimes did not always exactly follow that sequence (observable in the psychologically healthy), and that there might arise what he called 'disordered variants':

Psychologically they result in a bereaved person's capacity to make and maintain love relationships becoming more or less seriously impaired or, if already impaired, being left more impaired than it was before. Often they affect also a bereaved person's ability to organize the rest of his life.[5]

Other current theories of the process of loss and bereavement stem, to a greater or lesser extent, from these, and are variations on them. They all apply not only to bereavement from death, but to other life events which occasion significant loss: moving house, job loss, retirement, children leaving, and separation and divorce.

The Canadian, **Jean Monbourquette**[6], writing on coping with the losses and difficulties of life, says his own clinical practice and research have led him to formulate eight stages in coming to terms with the pain of loss:

- shock ;

- denial;

- expressing feelings;

- realizing the tasks of bereavement;

- discovering sense in the loss;

- forgiveness;

- 'inheritance' (subsuming the good qualities of the 'lost' person or relationship into one's life);

- celebration of the end of mourning and the beginning of a new life.

Simone Katzenberg[7], a matrimonial solicitor, practising in London and herself divorced, has written out of her own personal and professional experience on what she considers to be the emotional process to be worked through. She lists:

- breakdown;

- shock;

- anger;

- pain;

- hatred;

- grief;

- acceptance.

The basis of similarity which underpins these formulations of the grieving process helps us to see that there are certain elements which are common to all reactions to loss and life transitions, and in which we can identify our own emotions which—although worked through in a way unique to ourselves—are universal.

1. Arnold van Gennep, *Les Rites de Passage (The Rites of Passage)*, E. Nourry, Paris, 1907.
2. Elisabeth Kübler-Ross, *On Death and Dying*, Routledge 1995 (© Elisabeth Kübler-Ross 1969).
3. Elizabeth Collick, *Through Grief: the Experience of Bereavement*, Mirfield Publications, 1982.
4. John Bowlby: *Attachment and Loss Volume 1: Attachment, Attachment and Loss Volume 2: Separation: Anger and Anxiety, Attachment and Loss: Volume 3: Loss: Sadness and Depression*, Penguin Books, © The Tavistock Institute of Human Relations, 1980.
5. John Bowlby, Loss, *(see note 4)* (Penguin Books, 1991), page 85.
6. Jean Monbourquette, *Aimer, Perdre, Grandir*, Bayard Editions/Centurion, 1995.
7. Simone E. Katzenberg, *The Seven Stages of Divorce*, Solomon Taylor and Shaw © 1996.

Further reading

Practical Help

The 'Which?' Guide to Divorce, Helen Garlick, Which? Ltd, 1996.
The Divorce Handbook, Fiona Shackleton and Olivia Timbs, Thorsons, 1992.
How to… Survive Divorce, Roy van den Brink-Budgen, How To Books Ltd, 1995.

Marriage breakdown and divorce

Marriage Inside Out, Christopher Clulow and Janet Mattinson, Penguin Books, 1989.
Marital Breakdown, Jack Dominian, Penguin Books, 1968.
An Introduction to Marital Problems, Jack Dominian, Fount Paperbacks, 1989.
The Seven Stages of Divorce, Simone Katzenburg, Solomon Taylor and Shaw, 3 Coach House Yard, Hampstead High Street, London NW3 1QD, 1996.

Emotional and behavioural systems

Why Am I Afraid to Divorce?, Jane Butterworth, HarperCollins, 1994.
Why Am I Afraid to Tell You Who I Am?, John Powell, Harper Collins, 1969.
Why Am I Afraid to Love?, John Powell, Argus Communications, 1967.
The Art of Loving, Erich Fromm, Unwin Paperbacks, 1975.
Families and How to Survive Them, Robin Skynner and John Cleese, Mandarin Paperbacks, 1983.

The Presenting Past, Michael Jacobs, Open University Press, 1985.
The Marriage Work-Out Book, Mary Kirk, Lion Publishing,1996.

Violence

Love lies bleeding. When intimacy turns to abuse, Trevor Stammers, Hodder and Stoughton, 1996.

Being single again

Becoming Single, Hamish Keith with Dinah Bradley, Pocket Books, 1993.

New relationships

Divorce and Separation, Everywoman's Guide to a New Life, Angela Willans, Sheldon Press, 1994.
Before you love again, John Hosie, Millenium Books, 1993.
The Relate Guide to Starting Again, Sarah Litvinoff, Vermilion, 1993.

Children

Stepfamilies, Merrilyn William, Lion Publishing, 1995.
Parenting Threads—Caring for Children when Couples Part, ed. Erica De'Ath and Dee Slater, Stepfamily Publications, 1992.

Useful addresses

The national or London address is given, from which contacts for other parts of the UK and local branches can be obtained.

ASIAN FAMILY COUNSELLING SERVICE,
74 The Avenue, London W13 8LB
Tel 0181 997 5749

THE ASSOCIATION OF SEPARATED AND DIVORCED CATHOLICS,
c/o Cathedral House, 250 Chapel Street, Salford, M3 5LL
National Helpline 01706 352925

THE BEGINNING EXPERIENCE,
1 Apple Tree Walk, Climping, West Sussex BN17 5QN
Tel 01903 722230
Provides support, and a programme, for coming to terms with grief and loss, and shutting the door on the past. For separated, divorced and widowed and their children.

THE BRITISH ASSOCIATION FOR COUNSELLING,
37a Sheep Street, Rugby, Warwickshire CV21 3BX
Tel 01788 578328

THE BRITISH ASSOCIATION OF PSYCHOTHERAPISTS,
37 Mapesbury Road, London NW2 4HJ
Tel 0181 452 9823

FAMILIES NEED FATHERS,
BM Families, London WC1N 3XX,
Tel 0171 613 5060
Information Line: 0181 886 0970

GINGERBREAD,
16-17 Clerkenwell Close, London EC1R 0AA
Tel 0171 336 8183
Support organization for single parents and their families.

JEWISH MARRIAGE COUNCIL,
23 Ravenshurst Avenue, London NW4 4EE
Tel 0181 203 6311
Get advisory service 0181 203 6314
Crisis Helpline 0181 203 6211 or 0345 581999

MARRIAGE CARE (FORMERLY CATHOLIC MARRIAGE ADVISORY COUNCIL),
Clitherow House, 1 Blythe Mews, Blythe Road, London W14 0NW
Tel 0171 371 1341
National Helpline 0345 573921

NATIONAL COUNCIL FOR THE DIVORCED AND SEPARATED,
PO Box 519, Leicester LE2 3ZE
Tel 0116 270 0595

NATIONAL COUNCIL FOR ONE-PARENT FAMILIES,
255 Kentish Town Road, London NW5 2LX, tel 0171 267 1361

NATIONAL FAMILY MEDIATION,
9 Tavistock Place, London WC1H 9SN
Tel 0171 383 5993

RELATE [NATIONAL MARRIAGE GUIDANCE],
Herbert Gray College, Little Church Street, Rugby CV21 3AP
Tel 01788 573241 (or local telephone directory)

SOCIETY OF ANALYTICAL PSYCHOLOGISTS,
1 Daleham Gardens, London NW3 5BY
Tel 0171 435 7696

SOLICITORS FAMILY LAW ASSOCIATION,
PO Box 302, Orpington, Kent BR6 8QX
Tel 01689 850227

STEP-FAMILY,
72 Willesden Lane, London NW6 7TA
Tel 0171 372 0844
Counselling 0171 372 0846

INDEX